ALSO BY ANNE LABASTILLE

Woodswoman

Woodswoman III

Women and Wilderness

Mama Poc

The Wilderness World of Anne LaBastille

Jaguar Totem

Woodswoman II

Woodswoman II

Anne LaBastille

AUTHOR OF *Woodswoman*

W·W·NORTON & COMPANY·*NEW YORK*·*LONDON*

TITLE PAGE PHOTOGRAPH: *Logs being towed to cabin site by canoe at Lilypad Lake.*

Copyright © 1987 by Anne LaBastille. *All rights reserved.*

Printed in the United States of America.

First published as a Norton paperback 1988 under the title *Beyond Black Bear Lake.*
Reissued 2000 under the title *Woodswoman II.*

The text is composed in Avanta, with display type set in Cactus and Centaur. Composition
and manufacturing by Haddon Craftsmen. Book design by Marjorie J. Flock.

Library of Congress Cataloging-in-Publication Data
LaBastille, Anne.
  Beyond Black Bear Lake.

  1. LaBastille, Anne. 2. Women naturalists—United
States—Biography. 3. Women conservationists—
United States—Biography. 4. Nature conservation.
5. Environmental protection. I. Title.
QH31.L15A324 1987   333.7'2'0924 [B]   86–8498

ISBN 0-393-32059-6

W. W. Norton & Company, Inc.
500 Fifth Avenue, New York, N.Y. 10110
www.wwnorton.com

W. W. Norton & Company Ltd.
Castle House, 75/76 Wells Street, London W1T 3QT

9 0

For all my pioneer friends:
Denny, Christine, Dan, Barbara, Ron,
Lois, Jon, Little Jon, Brenda, Allan,
Rodney, Sue, Bud, Nancy, Frank,
the little Zs, Judy, Aziel, Mike

Contents

From Author to Reader   15

1. West of the Wind Is Discovered   23
2. Further Interruptions   34
3. Pitzi   47
4. Condor   56
5. The Ponds   70
6. Death from the Sky   84
7. The Decision to Retreat   100
8. Big Brother Is Watching   110
9. Half a Haven   117
10. My Nuclear Winter   131
11. Thoreau II   143
12. Two Guides   154
13. Chekika   169

14. A Copycat Walden   185
15. Sauntering Around Lilypad Lake   200
16. Neighbors   213
17. A Wild Winter at West of the Wind   220
18. One Woman's Wilderness   232
19. Night Thoughts   242

From Author
to Reader

W **As I begin this book,** it's hard to guess what readers know about me already. So perhaps for the benefit of new readers I should say a few words here about my background and the events leading up to this book.

I wasn't born a woodswoman. In fact, I first saw the light of day in busy New York City and grew up in suburban New Jersey. My only glimpses of "wilderness" were at Girl Scout camp, Camp Fire Girls retreat, and the local golf course. My parents—a concert pianist and a language professor—did not even belong to the golf club, yet I spent more time playing there, in the roughs and nearby woods, than half its members.

From earliest memory I always wanted more *from* nature and *of* nature. Books and articles told me there were places untouched by human tinkering and habitation, places where wildlife roamed unmolested and foot trails wound for miles without encountering a person or building. Stories like *We Took to the Woods, Drift-*

wood Valley, Enchanted Vagabonds, Quest for the Lost City, Two in the Far North, Lady with a Spear, and, most of all, *The Yearling* fueled my desire to find true backcountry.

But for many years I didn't go farther than my suburban backyard. I yearned for a tent and pack yet had to be content with a treehouse in a white pine and lunch in a brown bag. At Christmas I asked my parents for stout boots and a .22 rifle—only to receive silk stockings and a dictionary. I was dragged to dancing school and art lessons rather than taken fishing and hunting. I dreamed and schemed of running away to become a wrangler in Wyoming or a trapper in Saskatchewan. But when a strong-willed mother states, "Girls don't go camping!" or "You mustn't walk in the woods alone," and "You're too young to learn to drive," what was a meek sixteen-year-old to do?

Perhaps my love for the outdoors and wildlife is a form of rebellion against this early suburban environment and parental protection. Then again, the lure of the wilderness and exploration may be in my genes. Somewhere, centuries back, I had an adventurous English-Yankee grandfather who made his fortune treasure hunting in the Caribbean. Also, there was an intrepid paternal French forebear who pioneered a plantation in the West Indies. I like to think their blood courses more vigorously through my veins than that of the plump, homey Dutch and German grandmothers on the other side of the family.

Heredity, genetics, early upbringing, and reading aside, for me the real introduction to and infatuation with wilderness came the day I accepted a summer job teaching horseback riding in the Adirondack Mountains of upstate New York. It was the first time I'd heard of these mountains. I was still a teenager and woefully unworldly. After what seemed an interminable drive up old Route 9 from New Jersey to the edge of the six-million-acre park, I arrived at the rustic lodge where I'd be working. There I met rugged Morgan Brown, the innkeeper, and saw the wild Adirondacks. I was simultaneously smitten. Morgan Brown was to become my lifemate (for a few years anyway), and the Adirondacks my lifestyle (forever, I hope). But all this is written in my first book, *Woodswoman.*

Soon I was settled in these mountains, exposed to the seasons, weather, people, wildlife, industries, economies, and wilderness within this beautiful park with its mix of private and public lands. Over the years I've gone from stable hand to hotel operator to cabin dweller. From college student to writer/photographer to ecological consultant. From suburbanite to Adirondack guide. These hills have given me a fitting place in which to live and work. Where else could a person write and contemplate in a log cabin beside a lake next to an immense wilderness tract yet be able to travel to Manhattan (the publishing Mecca) and to Washington, D.C. (conservation capital of the world), in half a day?

The Adirondacks also provide me and many others with a kind of "soul food," an inspiration that is ephemeral as dawn mist, yet enduring as granite. For example, when I dealt with summer hotel guests during my years with Morgan, I could see the benefits of the Adirondacks for them, escaping from the cities in which they lived. The hills and lakes brought an easing of tensions, a quieting of sounds, a relief from air and water pollution. Most of our guests felt great pleasure simply in starting a wood fire, either while camping or in their cottage fireplaces at the lodge. The fire was free. It smelled good, looked romantic, and was safe. Few of these people had hearths back in their urban homes. Far fewer had ever hefted an ax. The guests also enjoyed packing a picnic and heading for a different lake every day. While most of them did not engage in pure wilderness pursuits, they were close enough to the real stuff to be touched by its presence, its peace, its purity.

Later, as an Adirondack guide, I led (and still conduct) many weeklong wilderness workshops for various academic institutions.

Most rewarding have been those for women only. Often the women were new to backpacking and camping. They were full of fears and hesitancies. Some were flabby; some were fat. Many worked at sedentary jobs, wore high heels, and pounded cement sidewalks daily. All were seeking youthfulness, vigor, and good health. They wanted to return from their backcountry experience with greater stability and self-confidence. Some were fed up with the pretenses of their suburban lives. The wilderness gave them simple and natural benefits and reliefs, just by being *in it*, and more.

What the wilderness did for these women is remarkable. First, they came to value a place where they could go safely without fear of rape, robbery, or harassment. Secondly, the wild outdoors was a stage on which they could test their physical strength and practice new skills. I have seen exquisite moments such as that when a sixty-year-old grandmother went skinny-dipping (first time ever) with a flock of loons on a crisp dawn. And hours of courage when a college girl braved a twenty-four-hour solo campout despite nocturnal visits by a black bear. Also a leap of self-confidence when a woman who'd recently undergone a mastectomy learned to rappel down a cliff and conquer her fear of heights.

Living next to a state wilderness tract and owning my thirty acres of private virgin woodland and ponds have shown me how to respect and love land, to become a part of nature. That's something I never felt in New Jersey or New York City. Nor will the millions of people living in little boxes piled atop one another, or side by side by side, who never discover the out-of-doors.

As Aldo Leopold explained, "A land ethic changes the role of *Homo sapiens* from conqueror to plain member and citizen of the land community."

He didn't mean the farmers' grange, or the local fish and game club, or even the property owners' association. He was talking about the community of bullfrogs, barred owls, white pines, brook trout, deer mice, red spruce, clear lakes, gray rocks, and blue jays. I've joined this community, and it makes me feel humble, joyful, and protective.

You'll not find me putting pink flamingos on my lawn—much less growing a lawn here under my pines. I'll not introduce any exotic fish into my ponds or transplant rare plants in my woods. I don't cut straight, healthy trees or dead ones. The former make a good genetic source for future forests; the latter, cozy homes for wildlife. There are plenty of culls to take for firewood. Pesticides, fungicides, herbicides, insecticides, and all other suspect chemicals do not belong anywhere on my property. And I'll protest and deter anyone who tries to do so. I want every member of this little Adirondack community around Black Bear Lake—from ants to owls—to flourish naturally, myself included.

Living in backcountry has taught me not to meddle, except under crisis conditions. Nature is running its own show. Most things are proceeding at their own pace in a fairly orderly fashion. I shall leave ecological functionings alone, just as a wise doctor doesn't prescribe medicines for a healthy patient. Where and when ecological malfunctions occur and demand rapid action or gradual alleviation, in the case of forest fires, acid rain damage, toxic waste poisoning, or flooding caused by deforestation, then I believe people *should* lend a hand.

In this book I have a lot more to say than in my earlier one about current environmental problems and my interventions. For one thing, I am ten years older, and I've lived in my cabin for twenty years now. For another, I've traveled more widely and become more deeply concerned than before, even cynical, about the fate of our natural world. Lastly, I've learned to speak up and out. Part of my upbringing was being taught to be a "nice girl." This meant talking in a low, soft voice and not questioning adults or authority figures. As long as a grown woman stays a nice girl, she does not tackle controversial or disturbing subjects, and she will not write or talk with a strong pen or a loud voice. So readers may find I'm no longer a nice girl, not as much of a romantic or dreamer and idealist as I once was.

This, in a nutshell, has been my exposure to the outdoors. It may help explain how I became a woodswoman and why my commitment to the conservation of nature and natural resources is so powerful.

A number of good people helped to make this sequel to *Woodswoman* a reality. Heartfelt thanks are due to Carol Houck Smith, my editor; Pearl Hanig, my copy editor; Julian Bach, my literary agent; Ed Burke for photographic services; Susan Fenton and Clare Pelkey for expert manuscript typing; Dennis Conroy for assistance with photography and planning; Ruth Roach and Judy Kellogg for postal services; and Richard Terry for legal consultation and APA advice. A special word of thanks to Dr. Dan Odell, my literary guru, who first gave me a copy of *Walden*.

—*Anne LaBastille*

Beyond Black Bear Lake

Go up to the mountain, and bring wood, and
build the house; and I will take pleasure in
it, and I will be glorified, saith the Lord.

—Haggai 1:8

1

West of the Wind
Is Discovered

W *The delicate sound* of water droplets gently disturbed the warm hush of that Adirondack spring night. Drip-drip-drip. The noise was light as the peepers' trill, but oddly out of place. I laid down my pen beside the manuscript on my desk and glanced at Pitzi. His ears were erect, eyes wide open. We listened carefully as this strange sound wafted through the open window. What could it be?

My watch showed 11:45 P.M. The Adirondack sky was spangled with stars. No rain. Perhaps dew was dripping from the cabin roof? I checked that and the kitchen faucet—nothing. It was the month of May, still too early to attract summer folk. Only a few hardy souls were at their camps on Black Bear Lake. Then I heard Pitzi's low growl. Someone was definitely outside.

On instinct I guessed that a person was paddling quietly past my dock. The dripping sound came from a raised paddle. Swiftly I reached up and turned off my gas lamp, plunging the tiny log building into darkness. Moving by habit, I grabbed a spotlight and shotgun. Since an incident years before, when drunken hunters accosted me one night from the lake, I have always kept loaded firearms placed strategically around the cabin. Now Pitzi and I sped down to the shore.

Nervously I probed the black lake with the powerful beam. Tendrils of mist rose from the chill water. A trout poked its nose up to make a small circle on the still surface. Bats buzzed by erratically, hunting for insects. Suddenly I saw it: a slim canoe with one person in the stern, paddle poised, dripping water.

"Who's there?" I called out as my German shepherd broke the night silence with a ferocious bark.

"I'm looking for Anne LaBastille," came the muffled reply. "Where does she live?"

I peered into the gloom. "Well, you've found her, but what the hell are you doing here at *this* time of night? Who *are* you? What do you want?"

Without answering, the dim figure maneuvered closer. I was able to make out a slender, medium-size individual with a head of tousled curls. Was it a man or a woman?

"Please put down that shotgun so I can talk to you," "it" said apprehensively.

Warily I lowered the gun. Pitzi stopped growling. We waited. When the canoe was roughly ten feet away, the mysterious paddler said breathlessly, "I'm sorry to bother you. I had to drive hours to get here after work. I just finished reading your book *Woodswoman*. There's so much I want to ask you, and I want to see your cabin."

"At midnight?" I asked in astonishment. "This is a strange hour to go visiting. Up here folks make their social calls in the afternoon and don't sneak up on people. You gave me a scare."

"Oh, I didn't mean to," said the husky voice. "I guess I got carried away. You're my idol. I want to be a woodswoman, too."

I stared at the canoeist. Yes, it could be a female floating there in the mist. But what kind of woman would intrude like this upon another's home? Only a young one. I relented slightly. "There's no way I'm going to invite you, a total stranger, into my cabin at midnight. Why don't you come back tomorrow afternoon? We can talk then."

She nodded and said nothing.

"What's your name, and where are you from?" I asked.

"Christina. From Albany."

"OK, Christina. See you tomorrow," I said firmly. "Good night." Turning my back on this brash person, I whistled to Pitzi and started back to the cabin. I flashed the light behind me once to see if she'd gone. She was still there, a dejected slump to her shoulders, just as I'd left her. On impulse, I went back.

"Christina," I called, "I don't mean to be unfriendly, but no one's ever come to my cabin this way before in the ten years I've lived here. How did you even *find* me?"

"It wasn't easy." She grinned impishly. "But my parents have a camp not far from Black Bear Lake. They asked around for me." She shivered slightly in the chilly spring air.

Suddenly I decided to be more hospitable. "Why don't you come on up and have a cup of cocoa? And get warm."

Eagerly Christina paddled to the dock, jumped out, and tied up her craft. She followed me up the narrow path to West of the Wind and waited expectantly as I lit the gas lamps. Pitzi sniffed her over. Slowly she gazed around the three small rooms—my studio, kitchen, and front porch. Seeming to hold her breath, she took in the black Boston rocker, Navaho rugs, my littered desk, a red cupboard, gay Guatemalan Indian curtains, a guitar. Then she gazed at shelf after shelf of reference books and an array of photos on the log walls. Eyes asparkle, she let out a happy exclamation. "Oh, it's so much better than I imagined!" Carefully she reached out to touch the pelt of Mapuche, my beloved silver fox. "That was my favorite chapter in your book," she confided. "I cried so hard when you lost your wild pet."

I knew then that the young woman was sincere and I hadn't made a mistake to invite her in. I started the cocoa while she continued to look about. She even climbed the ladder to inspect my cozy sleeping loft filled with down pillows and comforters.

We shared hot chocolate in front of the Franklin stove, where I'd lit a small fire. This was my first encounter with a woman admirer, and I found it awkward to keep a conversation going as she hung on every word. It made me feel like an actress onstage. Finally Christina inquired about colleges where she could study to become an ecologist. I felt on firm ground again and showed her several catalogs. Perhaps I could help her with educational plans. We spent an hour discussing courses and careers. It was 1:30 A.M. when she left.

I accompanied Christina back to the dock and waited as she moved into the mist and disappeared. The sound of dripping water, first so sinister, now so friendly, diminished. Slowly the serenity of that spring night settled down again over Pitzi and me.

When I was sure Christina's canoe was gone, I went back inside the cabin and sat down at my desk. I began to ponder the whys and wherefores of this odd meeting. Would other people try to find West of the Wind? In my willingness to write about nature and my life in the Adirondacks, was I opening myself up too much to the public? Was that precious privacy and sense of solitude—so important to a writer—to be shattered? Should I graciously open my cabin door to anyone and everyone who read my book? Or not?

The answers were slow in coming and never clear-cut. As time went on, there were occasions when I simply had to shoo visitors away. One morning, bikini-clad, I was sitting on my sun deck and energetically typing an article. The deadline was only a few days away. Ruby-throated hummingbirds kept me company, hovering

A cozy corner at West of the Wind, overlooking Black Bear Lake.

nearby from flower to flower in my deck boxes. They were as busy as I, making their living. Purple finches sang prettily from atop the balsam firs. The blackflies were kept at bay by hot sun and a brisk breeze. It was a perfect place to work. My fingers were flying when Pitzi barked in warning.

I looked up, and through the balsam branches which shelter my cabin from the lake, I could see a man in a kayak approaching. I knew nobody with such a boat. It had to be a stranger. I shrugged into a shirt and strode barefoot down to the water. The moment he saw me the man paddled faster, practically crashing into the dock. He was ready to leap out when I said coolly, "May I help you, sir?"

He sat down, surprised, and eyed me up and down, spending longer than necessary on my bare legs. "You're Anne LaBastille, aren't you? I've found you, haven't I?" Without waiting for an answer, he grabbed a fistful of topographic maps and a knapsack. Again he started to get out of the kayak.

"Wait a minute," I said sternly. "I don't believe we've been introduced."

"But I've been looking for you for a year and a half. Look at these!" He shook his fist. "I bought every fifteen minute topo map in the Adirondacks to locate this place. Now I want to see your cabin."

Something about his arrogant manner and bold eyes put me off. I resolved not to let him set foot on my property, even if he had purchased all two hundred quadrangles which cover the Adirondack Park. I thought: What if I showed up at some writer's apartment in New York City, brandishing maps and demanding entry? The writer would slam the door in my face and call the police. I couldn't do that here because I had no buffer. I had no doorman, secretary, or receptionist; no answering service; no one to fend off people. Only Pitzi and watchful neighbors scattered around the lake kept taps on me. Keeping calm, I asked the man how he had managed to discover West of the Wind.

"I took little clues out of your book and plotted them on the maps. Then I drew a big circle, and figured you lived within it" he explained proudly. "I was determined to find you."

"Really? Then what?"

"I drove up and went to several bars inside that circle, always asking if anyone knew you. Eventually someone told me that you live on Black Bear Lake. So here I am. Isn't it great? Don't I get to come in?" He grinned like a puppy who'd found a big bone. Obviously he expected to be praised.

"No. I think it's awful. Don't you have any sense of other people's privacy?" Then I told him that my work necessitated regular office hours, even in a cabin, and that I was facing a tight deadline. Apologizing, I said I couldn't ask him inside my house.

"Not even a glimpse?" he wheedled.

"No," I replied.

Shoving his knapsack and maps under the kayak deck, he

Pitzi and I relax on the sundeck at West of the Wind.

shook his head in disbelief. "Bitch!" he muttered as he flailed furiously down the lake.

The next few summers brought more intruders. Some were nice; others were positively brazen. One August I left Black Bear Lake for a week to attend a conservation meeting of the National Wildlife Federation. To my delight and pride, I'd just been appointed a director-at-large. During this period a woman walked around my lake with two dogs. She had apparently asked dozens of summer neighbors where the cabin lay. Once there, she settled down to wait for me, erecting her tent on a small knoll and setting a telescope on the dock. Here she sat much of the day, watching for my return. Curious (yet cautious) neighbors approached her and asked what she was doing there. (This is a survival system, like a "crime watch," we all practice on Black Bear Lake to protect one another.) The stranger said she had read my book, was a friend, and was waiting. Not sure what to do and not wishing to offend a real friend of mine, the neighbors backed off. But they and the mail boat driver continued to keep an eye on the place. On the second day they suggested that the woman leave as I might be away some time. But she and her animals stayed in the area for five days, and then she left. We missed each other by two hours.

When my neighbors told me of the incident, I could think of no one who would take such liberties. Moreover, the short note the woman left was not signed by a name I recognized. I was incredulous. Good thing we hadn't met, for I would have sent her and her two dogs packing!

The lake's "early-warning system" brought me word of another would-be searcher one morning. A friendly neighbor cruised up to tell me that an older man was sitting in his car in the parking lot at the public landing, asking anyone who came by when I might show up. "Looks like he plans to stay for a while," said my friend. "He's got magazines and food with him, and the car has out-of-state plates."

"What does he look like?" I asked.

My friend described a trim, clean-cut man, in outdoor clothes, about sixty with gray crew cut and mustache. At least he didn't sound like a kook. I thanked my neighbor and returned to work. What should I do? If I stayed home, the man might eventually beg a ride by boat or bushwhack in. If I took time to go out and meet him, it would interfere with my writing. I grimaced. Why did these things have to happen?

The thought of the waiting stranger niggled my mind all morning. While lunching on the sun deck, I half expected to see him pop out of the woods. Finally, by late afternoon, I decided to confront him and get it over with.

As I pulled up to the landing in my small aluminum outboard motorboat, a tall, erect man stepped up to meet me. "You're Anne," he said warmly. "At last!" Then he thrust a bottle of Wild Turkey, a huge watermelon, and a stack of magazines into my arms. "These are for you."

Hooking his thumbs in his jeans, he began explaining about the gifts. "I know you like a sip of whiskey once in a while when you're camping because you said so in your wonderful book. The melon's for a picnic at the cabin. And these magazines," he continued pleasantly, "each have an article you've written. You see, I've been following your work for a long time. I'd be most appreciative, ma'am, if you'd be kind enough to autograph them. Oh, and your book, too. It's in the car." He ducked back inside the car, then added *Woodswoman* to the overload.

"No," I sputtered, shoving the whole conglomeration back in his hands, "I won't accept these things. I don't *know* you. I refuse to take presents from a strange person."

Now it was his turn to be flustered. A flush rose on his cheeks, and his jaw muscles flexed. For a second I thought he might strike me—or cry. I wasn't sure which. We stood like two statutes in the empty parking lot.

"I see I've overdone my greeting," he said quietly. "But where

I come from folks are a mite more cordial. I do apologize, ma'am. I had been looking forward to meeting you for such a long time. Your book went straight to the heart of an old woodsman."

I glanced at his license plate—Louisiana. Southern hospitality. I gulped. Yankee reserve. The blush that hit my face must have equaled his, and I suddenly felt like an ungrateful wretch.

He went on politely. "I've spent my life hunting, fishing, flying in and out of wild areas. So now you know how much I appreciate your writing. Oh, yes, let me introduce myself. I'm Commodore Dace, U.S. Navy, retired, at your service." He gave a courteous bow.

Hoping I could salvage the poor man's pride, I extended my arms again and finally accepted all his gifts.

We spent the next hour chatting and laughing over my bad behavior and Adirondack life in general. Commodore Dace held no grudges. He told me war stories as I autographed his collection. We parted friends. Every summer or two he shows up at the landing and sends word up to me. I cruise down, and he bestows another bottle of Wild Turkey on me. A gentleman to the core, he's never even asked to see my cabin.

The most bizarre interruption to tranquil woods life happened one day while I was in my outhouse. The view from the seat is splendid. Right in front of the door a magnificent white pine towers almost a hundred feet high. This is the same pine I hugged and first felt the amazing transfer of energy that can take place between human and plant life. This is the pine that I still embrace as I gaze up at its tremendous heft, which sways sinuously in a storm. This is the pine beneath which I want my ashes strewn someday. I usually spend a little longer than necessary in the outhouse, simply to admire the sheen of the sun on green needles and the furrowed stout trunk.

I was doing just this early one morning when I saw an enormous black man with a halo of frizzy hair walk underneath the tree! Unable to believe my eyes, I sat riveted to the "throne." It is rather unusual to see black people, or other minority groups, in the Adirondacks, even today. In fact, I was the first camp owner on Black Bear Lake ever to invite a black woman here. It was 1966, and the event caused considerable comment.

This massive black man did not see me and walked nonchalantly straight for the cabin. He wore a red sweatshirt and had a camera around his neck. My predicament was both alarming and embarrassing. I couldn't stand up and pull on my pants without being seen. And I certainly did not want to confront this stranger while sitting inside my outhouse! What to do? When he disappeared around the front of the cabin, I made a ministreak through the woods for the dock. There I composed myself and nervously waited near my boat.

Eventually the man came down the path to the dock, taking photos here and there. Politely I asked him what he wanted and if he realized he was trespassing. He eyed me and said something I couldn't understand. I repeated myself. Again his reply was incomprehensible to me. With that, he waved good-naturedly and ambled slowly back the way he'd come.

I leaped into the boat, motored over to my closest neighbors, and burst in to describe this incident to them. Sally and Sid were as bewildered as I.

Then the mail boat driver brought us amazing information. The man, apparently a native of the Fiji Islands, was visiting a family who had a camp near our public landing. They had lived overseas in government service and met this person. He had gone on a walk to get some pictures of the lake and forest to show back home. Without much English, and knowing nothing of American rules of trespass, he had wandered around the lake and onto my land.

For once someone had found West of the Wind who didn't give a damn about me.

2

Further
Interruptions

🐾 *Early in my cabin life* I'd established a pleasant and productive routine. Mixing work, play, and health care was easy in that setting. During the warm months I would climb down from my sleeping loft at six or seven each morning, take off my nightgown, and put a pot of espresso on the gas stove. Then I headed for the lake. No one was ever about, so I could skinny-dip without qualms. I began my dawn dips in the spring, as soon as the temperature of Black Bear Lake rose to fifty degrees Fahrenheit, and quit them in the fall once the water again hit fifty degrees.

Jolted half-awake by the tingling water, I would race for the cabin, breathing in the wonderful smell of bubbling coffee. My swim was timed to the espresso pot, and I immediately poured out a tiny cup of rich black brew and topped it with whipped cream.

A canoe is a good place to work on a sunny day.

This was the other half of my wake-up. Now my mind was stirring. I dressed, fed the dog, and sat down at my desk.

When I first started writing, I discovered an interesting metabolic pattern. Mornings are my best time for writing. Time at the desk or on the sun deck is the equivalent of an executive's hours in an office composing letters, writing memos, researching, and editing. However, instead of coffee breaks and committee meetings, my work is broken by such distractions as meeting the mail boat, tramping to the outhouse, putting fresh wood in the stove, or admiring the hummingbirds. I am alone with time yet never really alone. On sunny, calm days I may even work in the bottom of my canoe, floating on the lake. My portable typewriter just fits on the seat like a stenographer's desk. And a yellow pad works anywhere. No word processors for me! I want no machinery or electricity between my brain, hand, pen, and paper.

By 1:00 P.M. this burst of brain energy has faded as surely as an engine shutting down from full thrust to idle. Hunger pangs take over. After a light lunch of cottage cheese, lettuce, whole wheat bread, and apple juice, I feel restless and in need of physical work. The afternoon is filled with comfortable chores like painting the roof, chopping wood, fixing the boat or canoe, or clearing my woods. On rainy days I like to make giant bonfires and burn up dead branches. There are always new projects to tempt or social visits to make. Sometimes I just wander playfully in the woods with the dog, taking photos. Other times I go swimming.

Evenings are spent corresponding with friends, rereading manuscripts, editing pictures, or reading. I feel no desire for TV. In fact, I'd dread it as a mental morphine taking time from creative work.

This metabolic cycle repeats itself methodically every twenty-four hours. It is so predictable that I often describe it to students when I instruct photojournalism workshops. "Listen to your bodies," I urge them, "when you write." And usually half the class will admit there *is* an ebb and flow to their brains and creativity once they have gotten in tune with themselves. Maybe it's because writing is as much a conscious, thinking act as an unconscious, psychic endeavor.

The days fly by, blending one into another. I lose track of which date it is. The timepieces I go by are the trill of spring peepers giving way to the boom of summer bullfrogs; the sight of flickers sitting along the roadsides in early fall; the last wedge of geese to fly overhead; ice forming; ice breaking up.

These natural biorhythms became disturbed more and more by personal and professional intrusions late in the 1970s. In addition to uninvited people and strange mail, phone messages started to seep into my secluded world. Up until writing *Woodswoman*, I had handled all communication by letter. Anyone who wanted to contact me simply wrote a letter. I figured the world had worked this way for centuries and gotten along all right. Besides, the length of time for mail delivery has decreased dramatically. I often imagined how a young woman must have felt two hundred years ago in Boston waiting for a love letter from London to cross the Atlantic by sailing ship; it might have taken six months. Or a rancher living in Arizona Territory one hundred years ago who ordered a rifle from back East; between the trains and pony express he might wait a year. No ZAP mail or Purolator Courier in those days! No Federal Express! At least I could figure on no more than a week between getting and answering a letter within the States; perhaps three weeks with foreign mail.

Of course, getting my mail delivered to the cabin was a somewhat complicated procedure. Summer and fall a mail truck brought postal sacks from our small rural post office to the public landing at Black Bear Lake. There a mail boat received and delivered the mailbags around the shore. Daily Pitzi would prance down to get my sack and proudly carry it up to the cabin or sun deck. Depositing it carefully at my feet, he earned a cookie and praise. Truck, boat, and dog make an effective team.

But winter and spring, mail comes only as far as a few weathered boxes on the dirt road. I had to hike, snowshoe, or snowmobile down the ice to these boxes. Pitzi always ran alongside, covering five miles for my three. Crisscrossing the lake's surface, he'd find otter slides and air holes. He discovered red fox tracks and paused to mark *his* territory. Or if we bushwhacked along the shoreline, a snowshoe hare sometimes sprang out of hiding and leaped through the forest. My dog gave hot pursuit, only to end up belly-deep in snow or tangled up in witch hobble. He never caught up with one of these fluffy marshmallow bullets.

It was great exercise to trudge up and down Black Bear Lake with a toboggan and mail sack and backpack. But I resented the time away from my desk, especially if a recent blizzard made the round trip into a two-hour ordeal. When I began *Woodswoman,* the situation became unwieldy. Frequent consultations with my editor were necessary. Also, I was doing short-term consultancies from time to time for organizations like the Smithsonian Institution, Gulf + Western, International Union for Conservation of Nature and Natural Resources, World Wildlife Fund, and so on. Once or twice a year I might work as a staff ecologist aboard the MS *Lindblad Explorer* on its fabulous natural history tours. It became evident that I could not function professionally from such a remote spot with just a mailbag and a German shepherd, stout legs, and snowshoes. I really needed a telephone, even though I hate phones.

A few years before, an underwater phone cable and a power line had been installed under and around Black Bear Lake. I had resisted, rationalizing that I'd started without such conveniences and did not want or need them. But now I took semiadvantage of modern technology and had an answering machine installed in the camp of neighbors, which had a phone and electricity. That way I could get certain important messages quickly yet not impose on my understanding friends. I'd go visit once or twice a week, listen to incoming calls on the tape, and cluster up on outgoing calls. This routine also brought us the luxury of a good chat and

Pitzi keeps an eye out for beavers at sunset. Mailbox is at right.

cup of coffee. Through the sharing of my professional life with Sid and his wife, Sally, we became the best of friends.

Mail and phone calls increased after my book was on the market. At times Pitzi could barely carry up the mail sack. Often I spent hours smiling or glowering at the incredible array of letters. They seemed to fit into three categories: purely complimentary letters from appreciative readers, bizarre or provocative letters from peculiar people, and despondent letters from people who needed emotional support. At the start I felt it only courteous to answer every one. Yet this could take an extra hour or two each day and cost several more dollars a month in postage. I began to wonder if this was necessary or even wise. Some of my readers answered and reanswered until I realized I must put a stop to this kind of correspondence.

I did receive some amusing and generous letters, however. A

man from Peachtree Corners in Georgia wrote, asking me for a date. He wanted to meet in Atlanta and stressed that he asked out only women with Ph.D.'s. Then there was a woman in Appalachia who wanted me to come and hunt bear with her. She smoked a pipe, lived in the woods, and decided I was her "soul sister."

Gifts arrived. A grandmother in Saskatchewan sent me a marvelous book about early trappers in the north woods. I thrilled to the hardships of those men who really lived "back in the bush" and days from the nearest person. A blind minister sent me a canvas wood carrier he had painstakingly crafted. In his days of sight he had been an avid hunter and fisherman. He yearned for the woods. Since there was a braille edition of my book, he was able to read it and vicariously enjoy my experiences. A divorced woman who took heart from my own story of a broken marriage and construction of a new life baked me a huge fruitcake. She mailed it to: The Woodswoman, Black Bear Lake, Adirondacks Mountains, NY. By the time it had hopscotched from post office to post office within this six-million-acre park, the cake was pretty ripe. My postmistress sent me a warning note about a "queer-smelling" package. She refused to put it on the mail boat. Finally I picked it up in person. Gingerly I opened the box, took a whiff, and heaved it in the garbage can.

Gradually I narrowed my replies down to two kinds: to letters from young people interested in improving their education and from people who were hurting. From my isolated desk in the forest I reached out to advise young girls in college or the Peace Corps on choices in conservation careers. I often sent consoling but confidence-building messages to women my age who were going through divorces or dreamed of living close to nature. To all of them I wrote, "You can do it! Just start!"

Interestingly, very few letters came from men, but those that did were dramatic. A psychologist wrote. He sounded brilliant, empathetic, but bitter over a recent breakup with his fiancée. I tried to write something helpful. Maybe it worked, for his next letter was less gloomy. He was obviously an intelligent and responsible human being, used to dealing with tragedies of drug users, suicide attempters, and child beaters. Over the years we've become close pen pals. Occasionally he sends me boxes of chocolate, books of poetry, and funny cards. These are delightful frills which a woodswoman doesn't get very often, especially from someone she's never met.

Another man who wrote for advice was a surgeon whose twelve-year-old daughter was seriously considering suicide. Desperate to get her mind and energies into healthy channels, he'd given her a copy of *Woodswoman*. He wrote, asking me to autograph it for her and include a little note of encouragement. My heart went out to Daisy, and I answered immediately. To my surprise and delight, she sent back a thank-you note. Her words were few, but it was a beginning. Her dad kept me informed of her progress. Eight years later Daisy is a bright, attractive college student. In gratitude, her father has mailed me wonderful mementos —great T-shirts, a hunting knife, snake antivenom, and other items useful to a woodswoman. I've never met him either.

Along with such an assortment of mail, I had to cope with the phone machine. Sometimes messages disturbed my peace of mind or broke my routine. Once I found three calls from a woman who said she was a lab technician/mountain climber living in Kansas City. She gushed and raved about my book, said she wanted to meet me, and left a return number. I was puzzled how a total stranger could have obtained my neighbors' number since no more than twenty professionals had it—editors, photographers, ecologists. I decided not to call back.

A week later the machine held three more messages from her. This time she was even more insistent about coming to meet me at the cabin. She explained that we had so much in common with our backgrounds, parents, education, and so forth. I was amazed that a completely unknown person would make such demands. Yet I knew from experience the lengths to which some people went. I asked my neighbor what to do.

"Call her," Sid advised. "Tell her you're busy."

That turned out to be a *big* mistake. A shrill female voice answered the phone and began a nonstop conversation. When I tried to interrupt and find out how she'd reached me, she replied mysteriously, "From a scientist friend." I listened patiently as my neighbors eavesdropped. During the forty-five minutes that she rambled on, I learned all the problems of this woman's life and her intense desire to get away from it all. "You've got to let me come and see you," she repeated over and over. I worried about my mounting phone bill, not to mention the imposition to my friends. Finally Sid motioned for me to hang up.

I cut in and told the woman I was leaving on assignment and could not accommodate her. Hoping this was the end of it, I apologized to Sally and Sid and went home.

The following week there were more calls from this woman. "She must be sick" Sally surmised. "Don't call her again."

"But supposing she *comes* here," I wailed. "She sounded crazy enough. I'd better head her off."

This time I simply said that I could not take the time from my busy schedule to return any more calls. I hung up. My neighbors applauded my action and poured us coffee. "This is fascinating," Sid admitted, "but we're glad not to be in your shoes."

Something must have snapped after that, for in her next call the woman was filled with violence and abusive words. She claimed that I had betrayed her confidence. She whimpered that I was cruel and she hated me. My neighbors and I sat in stunned disbelief. I offered to take out the machine and not subject Sid and Sally to further annoyance.

"Don't be silly," Sid said. "I wouldn't miss this for the world. It's the most excitement we've had all summer. Sally likes it better than the soaps. Maybe I should start tours to see the Woods-woman!"

Fortunately the calls from the woman stopped, but there have been other scary phone calls. In fact, I once informed the police and all my neighbors after a man kept calling and calling and insisting on visiting. I spent a tense week, being very careful where I went and making sure that no one followed me. Nothing happened. But that incident decided me. I *never* answer calls from people who fail to introduce themselves and give very good professional reasons for calling. My neighbors say that it's boring listening to my calls now.

What do such visitors and callers hope to find when they search out the Woodswoman? I still don't know exactly, but I'm sure America is lonely. Americans are looking for identities. They want to attach themselves to authors, singers, actors, and TV stars. These searchers have fantasies. They need to sublimate to enrich their lives. They want to talk. Many are under the impression that I have nothing to do. Some must think I sit under my pine tree, writing poetry or playing the guitar. They don't know about the grueling self-discipline and constant juggling of time that being a free-lance writer and ecological consultant entails. Truly, a free-lancer's life is one of hustling and hassling. These people are oblivious of the burden of correspondence, travel, conferences, study, and workshops necessary for someone like me.

I recall reading that Thoreau was also beset by requests from neighbors. He wrote: "They do not consider that the wood-path and the boat are my studio, where I maintain a sacred solitude and cannot admit promiscuous company—. Ask me for a certain number of dollars if you will, but do not ask me for my afternoons."

Other dreamers feel they "own" my cabin *and* me after reading my book. Perhaps that's why they have no compunction about walking right in. In a way I understand. In 1971 I read Dr. Charles Reich's popular book *The Greening of America* and was greatly taken with this Yale professor's fine conservation ethic— so much so that I determined to meet the writer and do an interview for *Adirondack Life* magazine. Dr. Reich was reputed to have a summer camp in the Adirondacks, but he was as elusive as a mink. His publishers refused to give out information. I asked for his whereabouts from town to town. When, in fact, I finally stumbled onto the right hamlet, his neighbors would not divulge the slightest clue to where his cottage stood. It was the best-kept secret in town. So I stopped looking and sat down on the steps of the general store one Sunday morning, hoping he'd show up for the *New York Times.* It was a lucky guess. . . .

Yet, even after I'd introduced myself and explained my mission, I got nowhere. Dr. Reich did *not* wish to be interviewed or visited, and *that* was *that!* I was crestfallen. So I do understand the zeal and intimacy which grow in a reader after a book strikes a chord in that particular person.

As I see it, the problem is one of boundaries—the delicate line between social contact and solitude. Some people respect privacy; others don't. Europeans seem much more courteous about such matters than Americans. By my willingness to write about my life, I've created a two-edged sword. My readers nourish me through sales, yet they threaten to devour me with overattention.

I believe there'll always be times when I feel rueful and resentful toward intruders. I'll refuse to answer letters and phone calls or to invite people in. As people continue to come, I'll feel more distressed by personal intrusions, especially when my routine is disrupted. Productive writing is harder to accomplish when a part of me uneasily awaits the *next* interruption.

There will also be times when I'll cherish my readers and try to accommodate them, when we'll share a cup of cocoa and philosophize about life. But one thing's sure. Although the setting of West of the Wind remains the same, the ambience has changed. My cabin will never be as peaceful and private a place as when I first lived there.

One of the great white pines I love so much.

3

Pitzi

W *Through all these* interruptions and intrusions I felt protected and comforted by the presence of my huge German shepherd, Pitzi. On the basis of his behavior, and that of my subsequent shepherds, I believe the best companion a woman living alone in the woods can have is a dog of this breed. I have tried other pets—an onyx cat (Inca); a silver fox (Mapuche); local wildlife such as flying squirrels, deer mice, and raccoons—but none was adaptable to cabin life. Also, they afforded me no real affection or protection.

I obtained Pitzi shortly after I had hand-built my little log home. He was a sinewy black and tan shepherd, given to me as a tiny puppy while I was in Guatemala doing doctoral research in wildlife ecology. I smuggled him back into this country in a shoulder bag at five weeks of age. Together we shared many adventures,

Julie, a budding woodswoman, Pitzi, and I speed down the lake on a canoe-camping trip.

predicaments, and days on the trail and in canoes during my first decade at West of the Wind.

But at about ten years of age Pitzi began to suffer from the combined effects of dysplasia and arthritis (both are disabilities inherent to this breed). His joints would creak audibly when he sat down, jumped into the boat, or rose from his place by the Franklin stove. To ease this large dog's pain, I gave him Prednisone, a cortisone type of drug, which seemed to help. Encouraged by the reaction, I continued to take him on writing and camping trips.

Then came a new job with *National Geographic* magazine to cover the eight hundred-mile-long Ice Age Trail in Wisconsin. It meant spending more than a month there, exploring choice sections of this intriguing hike-and-bike path, which closely follows the edge of the terminal moraine. This geological relict was left behind by one giant lobe of the ice sheet which covered North America twelve to eighteen thousand years ago.

There was nothing terribly steep or demanding along the route, so I decided to take Pitzi with me. He'd be a great addition to the article and good company. Thus, on a sunny Sunday in August, I slipped him a tranquilizer, coaxed him into a large air kennel, and entrusted him to American Airlines for the flight to Chicago. I was on the same plane with him, yet my heart was filled with apprehension the whole way. What if the temperature or pressure failed in the cargo section and I found a frozen dog at the airport?

No such horror occurred. But when I picked Pitzi up, he was as woozy as a surgical patient after an operation. I made him comfortable in a rented station wagon, loaded my camping gear, and headed for Milwaukee in ninety-five-degree temperatures. I flicked on the air-conditioning. Pitzi slept all the way. The next day he seemed almost steady on his feet. It looked as though we could hit the trail.

Pitzi, the *Geographic* photographer, and I crisscrossed the state, sampling sections of the Ice Age Trail from Lake Michigan to the St. Croix River bordering Minnesota. We saw bloodred sunrises, shimmering blue kettle holes, burgundy cranberry bogs, and deep hardwood forests. Day after day the brutal heat persisted. Day after day Pitzi stoically refused to eat and barely drank. Whether it was the aftereffects of the tranquilizer, his hip pain, or our constant movement, I wasn't sure. Finally I sensed that my dog was close to a breakdown. In desperation I pulled into a veterinarian's office late one afternoon and pleaded with him to look at my dog.

His condition was bad. The doctor flashed me an indignant look and immediately began intravenous feeding of fluids, antibiotics, and vitamins to pull Pitzi out of his dangerous dehydration. Then he sat down and gave me a good scolding for pushing Pitzi so hard. Within forty-eight hours this wonderful veterinarian had Pitzi back on his feet. From then on I took it much easier. The heat broke. Soon the story was done, and we were able to fly back home to familiar surroundings.

When the story appeared, there was a photo of Pitzi in a double-page spread. He sat in the bow of a canoe awash in golden sunlight, tawny as a lion, majestically guarding me as we drifted down the Wisconsin River. I cherish that picture; not every dog becomes a "centerfold." Yet I also get a twinge of remorse, remembering how close he came to death while that article was being researched and written.

The following summer was Pitzi's last. I was attending a monthly meeting of the Adirondack Park Agency. (This is a state land use planning group, which oversees private lands in the park.) I'd recently been appointed one of its eleven commissioners by the governor of New York State. It was a beautiful July day. We conducted part of our business out on the lawn around our offices in the sunshine. My dog was tied to a tree. Between committee meetings we took a midafternoon break. I unclipped

Pitzi's leash to let him run and ambled over to my pickup truck, parked under shady maples beside a town road. As I reached into the truck camper to get Pitzi's water dish, I heard a car racing down the road at high speed. Instantly I whirled to whistle since Pitzi had never become traffic-conscious. He was nowhere to be seen.

Two teenagers streaked by in a car going sixty miles per hour. A moment later came the screech of brakes and a horrible thud. Pitzi lay in the road. I raced to his side. A huge groan escaped his lips, and his entire body heaved. In that split second I lost control. Loving that dog as I did, I became hysterical. Screaming for help, I threw myself over his body and tried to raise his head. Members of the Park Agency flocked toward me. The culprit car shifted gears and roared away, flinging dust and pebbles over Pitzi and me. Somebody said, "You've got to move out of the highway. You'll get hit, too."

The dog continued to twitch spasmodically. "Don't move him," I shrieked, "until we know what's wrong. Somebody open up the truck and fix a bed for him. And make a stretcher. Hurry! I've got to get him to a vet. Please!"

Ignoring me, two of my colleagues yanked me to the shoulder of the road. Then they took hold of Pitzi's four legs as though he were a dead deer and hauled him up into the back of the truck. I could only think they wouldn't have done that to a human being. Any movement that stretches the neck or spine could snap the cord and cause paralysis. Maybe it did. I'll never know.

Desperately hoping that Pitzi was still alive, I cushioned my dog's body as best I could and leaped into the cab. My colleagues would call ahead to the nearest vet, fifty miles away. I drove those tortuous mountain roads at seventy-five miles per hour, not caring what chances I took on hills and curves. I thought of the two boys and car that had hit and run. My fists clenched at the thought of what I would do if I could find them.

When I squealed into the vet's parking lot, he was waiting. He took one quick look and shook his head. "He's gone, I'm afraid," he said gently. "You couldn't have saved him. The massive blow of the car must have killed him outright."

"But he kept twitching," I said insistently as a wave of grief swept over me. "I thought he was still alive."

"No, that was just nerve reflexes. Do you want me to dispose of the body?" he asked kindly.

I looked at the vet through eyes swimming with tears. So sure was I that Pitzi would survive that I'd never considered this next step. My answer came intuitively. "No. He belongs at the cabin. I'll take him there. Thanks, Doctor, but I'd rather take care of this myself."

I drove away with my tragic cargo, scarcely aware of where I was going. A small voice of reason finally whispered, "Stop, think, rest. How will you manage this?"

On impulse I turned into a motel. It was 4:00 P.M. and scorching hot—just as it had been that past summer in Wisconsin when Pitzi got sick. I walked to the rear of my truck and looked in the camper. My dog lay as if in sleep. Eyes closed, not glazed and staring. No drop of blood anywhere. I just could not accept the fact that he was dead. I laid my hand on his rib cage, waiting for a heartbeat.

Instead, a small, ugly, shiny fly buzzed up and settled on Pitzi's nose. Instant revulsion flooded me. Flies! They knew the dog was dead. They'd swarm in, cover him, and lay eggs. He'd start to crawl with maggots! He'd begin to stink in this heat. I tried to move the dog back from the window out of the sun, but rigor mortis had set in. Weighing almost eighty pounds, and as stiff as a board, he wouldn't budge.

This sobering encounter cleared my mind. I walked to the motel office and paid for a room. Immediately I picked up the ice bucket and then located the ice machine. Luckily it was early enough that the motel guests had not yet begun their cocktail hour. The ice bin was full. I began carrying bucket after bucket out to my truck. When Pitzi was completely covered with cubes, I allowed myself to collapse on the motel bed. At least my pet would be somewhat preserved until I could bury him.

Help. I needed a strong friend. Someone who could take the time to come to the cabin with me. A sympathetic person who would help carry my dog home and help dig a grave. With some trepidation, I began making calls. No one answered. I racked my brains for the homes of acquaintances within a fifty-mile range, or an hour's drive, of the motel. I was almost one hundred miles away from my cabin, in strange territory. However, I realized I wasn't that far from the small city where I had been hospitalized a few years back after breaking my pelvis in the woods. I'd made friends with some of the nurses in the hospital and, of course, had gotten to know the physician assigned to my case. In fact, "Dr. Mike" had become my regular M.D., and we called each other by our first names.

He was a cheerful, older, caring man, an understanding, hard-working surgeon, with a large practice. He was always willing to go that extra mile to help his patients. Now I reached out for his aid. Would he come to my rescue when it was my heart, not my bones, that was broken?

I dialed the number and learned that office hours were still in progress. But Mike offered to drive to the cabin with me after 6:00 P.M. I waited in the motel, alternating between pacing and crying. Two hours later Mike arrived. I checked out, and we started with two cars on the long drive. It took extra time. Tears kept blurring my vision. When I had a crying fit, I'd pull over to the side of the road. Mike waited patiently, coming over to the truck to offer me Kleenex and pat my back.

At sunset we reached the landing at Black Bear Lake and tried to lift Pitzi into my boat. He was cold and rigid, and it was incredibly difficult to place him in the bow. His legs stuck grotesquely up toward the sky. I thought of the hundreds of times he had whizzed down the lake standing up forward in the boat, head held high, tail and ears flattened by the wind, body arched as gallantly as a brigantine's bowsprit.

At my little dock we hauled him out and slid his body along the gravel path toward my cabin. It was almost dark. "Go to sleep," Mike suggested. "You've been through a lot and need to rest. I'll give you a sleeping pill. And I'll cover the dog with more ice. You can't do anything tonight."

I shook my head. No.

"Tomorrow you'll feel better," he continued soothingly. "I can take your boat down now and come back in the afternoon to help bury Pitzi. It's Saturday, so I don't have office hours."

No, I thought again. Tomorrow I would feel only worse. But it wasn't right to hold Mike there any longer. He had a two-hour drive ahead and professional obligations. I would have to handle the burial alone. We got back in the boat, and I took him down to the parking lot and his car.

As I cruised slowly back to the cabin, I realized this was the first time in twelve years that I'd been without Pitzi. I could barely stand to return to my home, thinking of what awaited me. As I trudged up the narrow path, I could see that large lump lying on the ground. There was no way I would sleep until Pitzi had been put to rest.

So, at 10:00 P.M. under a full moon that filled my fir forest with sinister shadows, I fetched a shovel and began looking for a grave site. I tested the ground a dozen times, trying to find an open spot under the trees without too many roots. I wanted my dog near enough to the cabin so I could see his grave from the sleeping loft. At last I selected a site and began digging. Pitzi was a large dog, and he needed a large hole. I worked down to hardpan (about three feet deep in Adirondack soil) and hacked through several roots to clear a space five feet long by about three feet wide.

Suddenly the thought of bears came to me. I remembered that they eat carrion and will scavenge for dead meat. What if a black bear smelled the dog and dug him up? The ghastly thought of Pitzi's remains in the jaws of a big boar bear or bones strewn throughout the woods was appalling. I got a pickax and deepened the hole. Midnight came and went. Barred owls hooted mournfully. Bullfrogs croaked. The air was strangely still. I worked on until 2:00 A.M. with no light but the moon.

Satisfied at last, I searched the cabin for a shroud. Pitzi had never lain on a special blanket or bedding. He just slept on my Navaho rugs or bearskin. Finally I chose my lumberjack shirt— the same one I'd left for him at kennels when I had to go away on work assignments. I wrapped him in that. Skidding his stiff body over to the grave hole took all my strength. Then he was lying on the bottom, next to the earth. I decorated his body with fragrant balsam branches, putting off the more serious and final covering.

With one last kiss and stroke of his noble head, I stuck my shovel in dirt and began filling the hole. When it was full, I heaped rocks on top. Later on I would landscape the grave with spruce log borders, gravel topping, five little fir trees, and a tombstone. For now all I wanted to do was keep bears out.

At last—at 3:00 A.M.—I was done. The task had helped tire me and drain the tension. More than that, I had brought Pitzi's life full circle. He had begun life here at five weeks of age; he had roamed these woods, left his territorial marks on many trees. Now he was part of my cabin, forest, and land forever. On inspiration, I found some citronella candles that burn for hours and lit them around the grave.

Up in the sleeping loft I could look out on their peaceful flickering. Sleep scarcely came that night, nor for many nights, as I mourned my pet. I kept a vigil with the candles burning for a month.

I never walk by the grave, even today, without wondering if Pitzi's bones and teeth gleam whitely inside a molding red and black wool shirt. Or if he's gone completely to nourish the five small firs above him and others in my forest. The tombstone reads "Pitzi." Someday there'll be another, and perhaps another, beside it. Those dogs, too, will join the endless cycle.

What remains, meanwhile, are the memories of a tawny gold shepherd beside me in the canoe, boat, truck, woods, and water.

4

Condor

Ironically, it was another *National Geographic* assignment that broke my siege of grieving over Pitzi. This time I was sent to Voyageurs National Park in northern Minnesota as part of a proposed issue on U.S. national parks. Again, it was a hiking, camping, and canoeing story. And, again, Pitzi would have gone with me had he been alive. I felt oddly incomplete without my furry "teammate."

Mike had been hinting that I should get a new dog. He'd called a couple of times, solicitously inquiring about my health, but I knew what was on his mind. Then, just before I was leaving, he tried again. Over the phone he said, "I've been reading about the German shepherds at New Skete Monastery near Cambridge, New York. Apparently, the monks breed, train, board, and sell these dogs. They sound excellent—good dispositions, country-raised, guaranteed free of dysplasia. Would you like to ride over and—"

Brother Job, my friend who raises German Shepherds.
Photo by Holly Caenazza

He got no further. "No way!" I burst out. "I don't want to *see* a shepherd ever again!" Tears sprang to my eyes whenever I thought of Pitzi.

"Well, sometime, somewhere you'll have to *look* at one," he retorted. "You can't go on mourning forever, Annie." Then he changed the subject, realizing how vulnerable I still felt.

In the back of my mind I knew Mike was right. Yet, with the flurry of preparations for my assignment, I thrust the problem away. Then, since the Albany, New York, airport was fairly near Cambridge, I decided to stop by for a few moments en route and see the kennel. A quick look could do no harm, I rationalized. Besides, Mike had sent me the news clipping, and I was curious to visit this isolated religious retreat. I followed a winding road through Grandma Moses farm country until it turned and became dirt. The way climbed higher and higher up a narrow valley bordered by old stone fences, abandoned fields, and gnarled apple trees. Around a curve I came upon a low, dark wooden kennel house and gift shop. Farther up the hill I could see a quaint Russian Orthodox chapel with eight golden onion-shaped spires framed by graceful paper birches.

I went inside the gift shop, where a young monk in the dark brown flowing robe of the Brotherhood of St. Francis greeted me. He had a reddish beard, warm hazel eyes, and an ingenuous smile. "How may I help you?" he asked softly. "I'm Brother Job."

He waited for me to speak. I could hear shepherds barking somewhere in the background. And then I just blurted out the whole story of Pitzi and of my own life in the woods. At the end I said, "Do you think I could take a peek at your dogs?"

"Of course," Brother Job said, leading the way to the kennels.

It's hard to explain to anyone who's not an inveterate dog lover how the sight of those beautiful shepherds tugged at my heart. There were sleek broad-chested males; shy glossy females; dozens upon dozens of plump puppies gamboling about the pens.

Each litter wore a distinctive colored ribbon, which denoted their ages, and a tag with one letter of the alphabet standing for their names. I admired a green set of As about four weeks old and a blue set of Bs at two months.

In the last pen, all alone, was one red C. He was the runt of that particular litter. All his brothers and sisters had been sold, but this one was a "reject." He was not "show quality" because one testicle had never descended. Otherwise he was perfectly formed. As I peered into the pen, a pair of enormous batlike ears perked forward, dwarfing the inquisitive little face. Four paddlelike paws, foretelling his future size, scrabbled at the wire. His fuzzy tan chest pressed against the gate.

The monk, who was also the trainer, opened the pen. Boldly the pup wobbled out to greet me and sat down between my boots. Looking fearlessly up into my face, he tugged at my jeans with pearly white sharp teeth. Then he rolled over and trustingly displayed his roly-poly belly.

I hesitated before bending down. Part of me said, "How adorable. How cuddly. It would feel so good to hold a dog in my arms again." Another part warned, "Leave! Don't get attached to another pet. It hurts too much." The first part won out, and I stooped down to pick up the puppy.

Brother Job nodded his head. "That would be a fine shepherd for you, Anne. He's very bright, sociable, strong. He loves to romp outside and would take to your type of life and woodland setting. As long as you don't want to show or breed him, he's as fine a dog as we have. I'm already attached to him."

Quickly I set the dog back down. "Oh, no," I said sadly. "I'm not interested. No animal could ever replace Pitzi. I'd feel as if I had betrayed him if I took another dog so soon anyway. You know," I explained, "people who lose their spouses don't rush right out and marry the next month. That's the way I feel about getting a new dog."

"Yes, I understand your feelings *now*," Brother Job said sympathetically, "but they may change *later*."

"I don't think so. Having a dog is a lifetime commitment," I replied. "At least for *its* lifetime. That's ten or twelve years with shepherds. I'd never take one just for a couple of years. It's a womb-to-tomb proposition. And it's the tombstone ending that I can't go through again."

"Of course," the monk murmured kindly. "Well, just think about it while you're away. He may still be here when you come back, although I doubt it. We have a waiting list of over a year."

As if to emphasize Brother Job's words, the precocious puppy whimpered and sat down on my foot. He seemed to like me. My heart went out to the little "orphan."

The *National Geographic* assignment was busy, and the surroundings were idyllic. Together with my guide and the contract photographer, we camped, canoed, shot aerials, and explored much of Voyageurs. The weather was perfect. Mornings dawned cool and mist-shrouded, with ravens and gulls croaking from the pines. At noon, hot sun and strong breezes danced over the lakes, frothing them blue-white. Evenings were still and star-embroidered as we sat around the campfire. I began to come alive again.

That mischievous puppy stayed in the back of my mind. Halfway through our assignment we came into International Falls to reprovision. The puppy became an insistent whisper. I called long distance to the monastery and made a tentative offer. "If I pay for the board and care of the puppy, could you hold him until I return?" I asked. "I'd like to look at him again. Maybe I can make a decision in a few weeks."

"Of course," Brother Job said. "Really, this is the ideal dog for you. He's shaping up so nicely, Anne."

When I returned to New York State in midfall, I was ready to see the scamp again. Before driving over, I stopped at Mike's office and told him the good news. "You were right," I said. "It's time for another dog. Want to come with me? After all, it was your idea to begin with."

This time there was little hesitation when the puppy and I met. His ears, bigger than ever, literally looked like wings as he raced across the floor to meet us. Brother Job and Mike exchanged looks as I scooped the puppy into my arms.

"He looks like he could fly with those!" I laughed. Turning to Brother Job, I exclaimed, "I'll name him Condor—after the Andean condor—the largest flying bird in the world." Abruptly I realized what had happened. The process of healing that had taken place at Voyageurs was complete. I *was* ready for a new dog.

We left New Skete that afternoon with a long pedigree, a list of instructions, and a book on dog behavior coauthored by Brother Job, *How to Be Your Dog's Best Friend.* There was also a large bill, but I hadn't paid it. My doctor had. He was determined I have a new companion, and money was not going to stand in the way. I was so touched by his generosity that I gave him (and his well-starched shirt) a huge hug. He froze for a moment in surprise, then hugged me back. For those brief seconds he let his professional reserve drop. What a very nice man, I thought, my heart full of affection.

On the way down that winding dirt road Mike's shiny car became coated with dust. The puppy got carsick and threw up over the seat. Finally he peed on the floor. The neat-looking Buick was a shambles. Back at Mike's office, where I'd left my truck, I offered to clean up his car at a car wash and also pay for the puppy. "He's so expensive," I groaned.

"Don't worry about it," Mike said. "Consider the expense as buying freedom from dysplasia. Your new shepherd will never have to go through the agony Pitzi endured in later life. That's one of the benefits of good breeding and careful bloodlines."

Transferring Condor to my pickup, I fixed him a little bed on the cab seat beside me. Then I stopped to buy puppy chow, canned meat, milk, and a rawhide bone. He seemed more comfortable in the bouncy truck than in the smooth car, so we arrived without a mishap at Black Bear Lake. Condor seemed scared by the next form of transport—my aluminum boat and outboard motor—because of the vibrations and noise. Then, finally, the puppy and I were home. He sniffed about the cabin, especially where Pitzi had slept and eaten. Then the pup sat down by the kitchen and eyed me expectantly. Supper was the only thing on his mind after that long, dizzying trip.

After the tired dog had eaten and fallen asleep on the bearskin by the stove, I examined his pedigree. My eyes roamed down the paper with its long list of sires and bitches. Suddenly I saw the name of what would have been the puppy's great-great-great-great-great-great-great-grandfather in Germany. *His* name was Condor! Serendipity.

Before long I took the puppy back to Brother Job for an in-house training session. I knew this tall, caring man would work wonders with Condor. In a little more than two weeks, while I was away on a consulting job, Job had him sitting, lying, staying, coming, fetching, and carrying. Having a superbly trained dog would make a big difference when I took Condor with me on assignment and to lecture.

I went to pick up the puppy at New Skete on a frigid, snowy January day. The scene that greeted me was like something from *Dr. Zhivago*. The brown-robed, bearded monk was standing in the snow like a youthful St. Francis, surrounded by shepherds of all ages and in all stages of obedience training. Some were sitting or lying quietly; others were being walked at heel position by other monks. A few were yipping with high spirits in the crisp air. Backdropping the open field was the little chapel with its gold spires glittering in the sunshine. The snowy roof edged with icicles made it look like a frosted wedding cake.

Condor must have become imprinted to me early on, for he never leaves my side except to chase squirrels and to piddle. A sweeter, more patient pet I never could have found. But when he rides with me in the truck, boat, or canoe or is in the cabin or tent, he is pure professional guard dog. Woe to any stranger who dares get too close to me at home or in vehicles. Condor is equally protective in the woods, so I have no fear about going anywhere alone.

Condor has copied Pitzi in several things. He totes my mailbag back and forth to the daily mail boat in summer. He has slipped up only twice. Once he dropped my bag off the dock into the lake at sight of a fluffy, white black-eyed Pomeranian female in the mail boat. Another time he buried the sack in the forest when I was late bringing a cookie to the door to reward his service. I spent *hours, days* combing the ground. I even asked a local water witch and clairvoyant for help, but we never found the sack.

Like Pitzi, Condor has clinched with porcupines. He's experienced one run-in and taken 27 quills in nose and mouth. I pray he won't match Pitzi's four encounters and total of 130 quills!

Condor is an excellent bear deterrent when we're backpacking. He chases them up trees with the same gutsy vigor that Pitzi had. The first bear he ever saw was in the parking lot at Black Bear Lake one spring afternoon. I was paying no attention to him as I loaded my boat with items from a long-overdue shopping trip. Condor started barking. I figured fishermen might be walking by. He kept on and on, until I looked up. No more than fifty feet from the dock a two-hundred-pound black bear was nosing toward the garbage Dumpster. In a flash my dog was out of the boat and after the bear. The animal streaked up a yellow birch and lodged itself in a crotch about twenty feet off the ground. Condor tried to climb up right after it. I hurried close up with my camera, eager to get a few frames. Condor barked harder.

A black bear in a yellow birch tree.

Then, to my surprise, the bear leaned *down* the tree, its front paws bracing it vertically on the trunk, and chomped its jaws together several times. Its teeth clattered ominously. It reminded me of a rattlesnake shaking its tail in warning. Then its throat swelled with a low growl. I sensed the bear was angry enough to come down after Condor. So I dragged him away and tied him in the boat. Seconds later the bear slithered down the birch with a great scratching of claws and a welter of fine bark shreds. It started toward us, then turned and ran into the woods. Condor kept up a frustrated fury of yelps until my outboard motor drowned him out.

My dog is a wonderful swimmer. He delights in pulling me into shore when I grab his tail in deep water. Someday he may save my life with this trick. On backpacking trips he carries his share of food, a can opener, and his bowls, plus an occasional surprise I throw in—like a bottle of wine. Once I loaded him up with a dozen long iron spikes which I found beside a trail bridge back in the woods. He clanked along for five miles behind me, throwing disgruntled looks my way.

The main difference between the two shepherds is that Condor minds beautifully and is more of a teammate, whereas Pitzi always had a stubborn and independent streak. Sometimes he just took off on his own business. Moreover, Condor is a bigger celebrity. While Pitzi appeared in a *National Geographic* "centerfold" photo, Condor has made it onto "The Today Show," "PM Magazine," and "Sunday Morning" TV shows, plus an "I Love New York" Adirondacks ad. His picture has been in many of my published articles. I keep telling him it's only a matter of time before Hollywood calls.

Condor is at his best in a canoe, sitting regally in the bow, sniffing the breeze. His weight helps balance the boat and hold it into the wind. Only once has he disliked canoeing. It happened when I took him to Florida to do a short article on canoe trails in

the Everglades National Park. Our first venture was through the mangrove swamps into Whitewater Bay. Before leaving, I had to obtain a backcountry permit for a campsite. The only one available was on a large wooden tent platform perched over a shallow, brackish bay. It sounded like a marvelous place to spend the night.

Our canoe path twisted and turned through narrow channels, marked only by numbered lengths of white plastic pipe stuck in the mud. One wrong turn, and you could be lost forever. Condor constantly had to duck low-hanging branches and spider webs as the canoe scraped between red mangrove roots and trunks. On some turns there was barely enough room to maneuver one-way. It took six hours to cover perhaps six miles, paddling, pulling, pushing, and poling.

By midafternoon I had passed only one spot of dry land—an island of hardwood trees about one-foot elevation above high tide. Condor took a rest stop there, and I ate lunch. Then we pushed on toward the camping platform. The sky was graying fast, and a stiff wind blew from the north. Obviously a cold front was whistling through. Since the sun had been blazing hot that morning, I had rigged up a parasol to shade the dog in the canoe. That further complicated matters as it kept blowing inside out.

When I reached the wooden platform, it suddenly dawned on me that there was no place for the dog to relieve himself. Now shepherds are fastidious to a fault. I doubted he would go to the bathroom on a planked-over platform, where nothing more was available than tents, an outhouse, poles, and a roof for shelter. Quickly I set up my one-woman, one-dog pop-up tent and laid out the cooking gear. Then we struck out to find firewood and a bit of dry land. Everywhere I looked, mangrove roots arched and tan-

Condor likes to see where we're going.

gled above the murky water. Twilight was coming. Paddling anxiously, I finally found a spot about three feet wide and fifteen feet long which was elevated. Clambering onto it, I tried to coax Condor to "do his duty." He wouldn't. The "island" was densely grown with an aspenlike tree. I crashed through a few feet, hoping the dog would follow me and find a trunk to his liking. Then abruptly I stopped. Something about the vegetation looked suspicious.

Suddenly I remembered. It was *poisonwood*. An old, unpleasant memory came back of a brush with this toxic tree in the tropics and the severe rash which followed contact. I crept back to the canoe, gingerly holding branches away from my face. I hoped Condor would not brush against any of the dangerous leaves and get the sap on his coat.

Back on the platform, the wind was gusting to thirty miles an hour. Dusk was gloomy. I realized it would be foolhardy to go out in the canoe again that night. Condor was in for a long wait. To try to solve his dilemma, I broke off a few nearby mangrove branches and set them up in the cracks of the platform like a bush. I put them near the outhouse. Maybe he'd get the idea.

Temperatures fell to forty-five degrees Fahrenheit that night, and I snuggled deep in my sleeping bag. At midnight there came a plaintive whimper. I struggled out into the frigid night and led Condor to his "bush." Nothing doing. Then I decided to use the outhouse, hoping the idea might transmit itself to him. Still nothing happened. We went back into the tent, my bare feet aching with cold.

At 5:00 A.M. I awoke to another soft whine. Again I took Condor to the appointed rest area; again without success. Then I recalled his habit of always marking his own scent on top of mine when I urinated in the woods. So after I piddled on the branches, I waited hopefully for Condor to show me *he* was top dog. My ruse fell flat.

A huge red sun rose at 7:00 A.M. It saw us pushing off from the platform bound for the poisonwood island. My poor dog could wait no longer. Once there, he leaped ashore and relieved himself several times while I cautiously crept after him, holding back branches so as to avoid contact.

Back home the only ill effects of this canoe trip was a tiny rash on my left foot and a quizzical look from my dog the next time he saw me lash the canoe atop my truck. What *now?* he seemed to be asking.

Aside from our canoe trips, the most companionable times with Condor are when I take him on lecture engagements. Since the publication of three books I find myself supplementing my free-lance income more and more by public speaking. Often I introduce the dog to the audiences or classes from the stage. Students love him. He's become a real ham, posing for pictures, accepting snacks at autograph parties and receptions. The one thing he doesn't like, however, is to hear people clapping after my appearance. Condor goes "bananas," barking and prancing like a wild animal. Who knows what triggers off his frenzy? I've written Job, asking his opinion. He thinks the noise might hurt his ears.

Or could it be that he's just envious that *he* isn't the center of attention?

5

The Ponds

🐾 *Henry Thoreau wrote,* "A lake is the landscape's most beautiful and expressive feature. It is the earth's eye; looking into which the beholder measures the depth of his own nature."

Thoreau had his Walden, his Flint, Goose, and White ponds, and he reveled in his walks and boat trips there.

Around my cabin I have a similar set of "Lakes of Light." Like Thoreau's, they beckon, intrigue, and delight me. Often in the afternoons, after writing, I walk to visit them, just as other people like to browse through favorite shopping malls or pay calls on special pals.

Closest to Black Bear Lake is Birch Pond. I can reach it in five minutes by threading along a faint fern-lined woods trail or in ten minutes by following the spoor of otters and beavers through the swamp which connects lake to pond. Fifteen minutes farther lies lovely Lilypad Lake. It is connected to Birch Pond by a tiny stream yet divided by two forested knolls. Around its serene surface lies wilderness—pure wilderness. From its wild shore I can hike in a figure eight: walk west to Sunshine Pond and wade on its minuscule sand beach or climb east up Sunrise Mountain to Eagle Pond. In both cases I can circle back to the cabin via little-used trails. One is very old. Snippets of this trail cross my property. It used to lead from Black Bear to a large lake five miles away where several hotels were once located. Sixty years ago summer folk would traipse from lake to lake on a Sunday, stopping at a rustic lodge to feast on tea, scones, and homemade pies. The owner then took them down Black Bear Lake in an ancient boat with a "one-lung" engine. At the landing they were met with horses and buggies and driven back to their respective hotels. Another trail takes me through an old lumberjacks' clearing, past a tumbled barn, and into a large beaver meadow.

None of my ponds is grandiose. Rather, they are small and humble. No tourist would go out of his or her way to visit them, nor would a fisherman cast a fly here. Why would they, when among the three thousand lakes and ponds of the Adirondack Park, one can be awed by Boreas Ponds, Elk Lake, or Lake Placid? Or happily hooked at Tupper Lake, the Saranacs, or Lake George? Yet to me my lakelets are as comfortable as good friends, each with its own personality and resident wildlife.

For years I simply walked, skied, or snowshoed to see them, skirting shorelines or crossing ice. In winter Birch Pond was transformed from a plain, brown-as-brandy, mucky-bottomed, narrow body of water to a silver-white crescent of crystal set between iced balsams. One Valentine's night I skied with Condor up its moonlit length and started across the small beaver meadow at its upper end. Delicate snow bridges spanned the still-flowing inlet. Cautiously I slipped over one arch, hoping it would bear my weight safely. It would not be healthy to crash through into the stream with skis on, get soaking wet, and then have to dash home in minus-twenty-degree temperatures. The first bridge held.

On the second, Condor dashed ahead and broke through. His hind legs plunged downward, but he twisted and lunged safely for the bank. On the third bridge the center plopped softly into the inky black water with a hiss before either of us could cross.

I retraced my ski tracks, etched like two ebony ribbons into the moon-glittering surface. The ice was two feet thick; the snow, twenty-eight inches. I passed a cluster of cutoff stumps poking up above the snow. This meant they'd been cut in winter years ago. I pictured a lone lumberjack snowshoeing up here with his woods horse, sawing the spruces, and dragging stout timbers back to his lodge for posts or pillars. The height of the stumps indicated that on that distant day the snow depth was three feet on the level.

These are the only trees I've ever seen cut on my entire thirty acres. The forest stands virgin and tall—never burned, lumbered, farmed, built upon, or pastured. The only other clue to human use is at a mossy seep that trickles into Birch Pond near the beaver meadow. In 1965, when I began posting my property lines, I found an old glass jam jar hung upside down on a branch over the seep. Digging gently into the ice-cold water and sphagnum moss, I discovered a "spring hole." Someone had laid a few smooth stones in the seep to form a drinking spot. The same lumberjack perhaps?

Once at Birch Pond I surprised a hooded merganser. The male preened quietly among a flotilla of cow lilies. His pure white crest and chest flashed in the late-afternoon sun, and his sleek body looked like black lacquer against the green pads. With his yellow eyes matching the yellow flowers, I was reminded of a Japanese painting: *Mandarin Duck Among Lotus Blossoms.*

Lilypad Lake is shallow and clear. It is nowhere more than ten feet deep, with a boggy edge, yet the shoreline has a symmetry that pleases the eye and calms the soul. I first camped there near the time of summer solstice. At dawn a giant tangerine orb trembled precisely in a cleft between the hills across the lake. It seemed a fortunate positioning of sun and landscape on the twenty-first of June. This lakelet has become my favorite. It is one of Thoreau's "God's drops."

On the old topographic maps of 1894 Lilypad shows up as two ponds connected by a narrow channel. On the 1954 quadrangles there is an hourglass-shaped lake. Evidently beavers dammed the outlet of the lower pond near the turn of the century, and the water rose a couple of feet. This was enough to create a lake. Subsequently many spruces and firs died along the banks and on both sides of the channel. Today the two phalanxes of dead stubs that march out from shore toward the center of the lake are a distinguishing mark of Lilypad.

Whenever I carried a canoe up there, I would paddle out among the stubs, admiring their silhouettes against the sunset and the texture of the weather-beaten wood. Once, paddling quietly, I came upon a young buck munching lily pads, hock-deep in water. The wind was in my favor, and the canoe pointed straight at him, so he didn't notice the intrusion. I could hear the water dripping from the pads and the chewing sounds he made as he slurped up the spaghettilike stalks.

There are no trails around Lilypad, yet strangely an "outlaw camp" once existed on the south shore. While posting my land one fall, I stumbled onto a wide sheet of black plastic pulled over some humps and bumps. It had been in place for months because hollows were filled with rainwater and greenish scum. Branches had fallen and poked through the plastic. I called it an outlaw camp because it was technically illegal. My back property line borders a fifty-thousand-plus-acre tract of wilderness—part of the one-million-acre wilderness system within the state's Adirondack Forest Preserve. By law no motorized vehicles, buildings, or roads are permitted there. Tents and campsites are limited to two weeks' use. This particular camp sat about a hundred yards within the wilderness and had been there a long time.

I yanked off the plastic and peered beneath, uncovering several pails and small drums. Excited as a kid on a treasure hunt, I started prying them open. Some held staples like flour, sugar, coffee, salt—mostly mildewed and rotten. Some had kerosene, matches, and rusty lanterns. Others clattered with heavy china, pots and pans. Two tattered sleeping bags were strewn on the ground. Evidently bears, squirrels, or raccoons had unearthed and destroyed them.

Over the weeks I toted this trash back to my cabin in a pack and out to the Dumpster by boat. From it I salvaged half a dozen cups, saucers, plates, and two skillets. I stored them away in a box, figuring someday they'd be useful.

Ever since I bought my land and first laid eyes on Lilypad, I had dreamed of having a tiny cabin here. It would be the ultimate in wilderness retreats because my "front yard" would face east, looking over the lake and wilderness area. As I'm the only private person with shoreline there and the rest belongs to the state of New York, *it's all mine* because I'm a resident of this state *and* a property owner.

However, logistics were difficult. Without any boat access, road, or trail connections, building a structure at Lilypad meant lugging everything needed on my back and bushwhacking more than half an hour. In the beginning I erected a tiny lean-to and camped there when time permitted. But Adirondack weather is too rigorous to allow more than five months' usage of an open camp. A little later I began the base and sides of a miniature cabin. But before long my career took over, and there was never time to finish it. So my dream languished at Lilypad Lake.

Sunshine Pond, a brief bushwhack from Lilypad, is a cheerful bit of "sky water." It always seems to be sun-sparkled and breeze-ruffled. Where the wind scours the shore, a croissant-shaped sand beach lies. I come here to swim because Lilypad is too shallow and soggy around its shores.

Sunshine was home to two herring gulls for years. Every summer I saw a handsome pair sitting on the large rock in the middle. It was whitewashed with their guano. I suspected they had a nest but never heard or saw chicks. Nevertheless, the gulls set up a raucous, anxious mewling whenever they spied me. Sometimes they would fly over Black Bear Lake, wheeling wild and white against the sun. Their cries would sift down, taking my thoughts away to the coasts of Maine or Florida, to salt-splashed rocks and mangrove isles.

Then came the year when only one gull visited Black Bear Lake. It came often, sat on a rock, seemingly lonesome and dejected. I'd pass by it on my sailfish or in my canoe, wondering if its mate had been killed overwinter. For three years it lived a stoical solitary life, never squalling as in the old days.

Finally, there were two again, cartwheeling and crying across the sky. I like to think the Sunshine Pond gull coaxed its new love to this unnatural yet heavenly gull habitat.

Only once did I portage my canoe to Sunshine—a hefty carry —and prowl its shores. Beaver signs were everywhere. I was sure a lodge and dam were up the inlet. Easing into the winding streamlet, I paddled quietly while my dog tested the air for scents. Suddenly I caught the flash of a scaly tail slapping water dead ahead. Condor began a barrage of barking in the bow. I froze and held my paddle motionless. A young beaver surfaced inches from my lower suspended hand. Its bright eyes stared saucily up at me, and its stiff little whiskers twitched. I had been reading the book about Paddy, the little beaver pet of a Canadian wildlife biologist. Impulsively I wanted to cuddle this one for a moment. I lunged for the small creature. My fingertips grazed its thick fur. It dived. It was my first feel of a wild beaver. Childish with delight, I half

---

OVERLEAF: Exploring a wilderness pond in an inflatable raft.

rose to plunge after it, then stopped. Which of us was more surprised, the beaver or I, is hard to tell.

Carrying canoes to and from my ponds was hard work. Moreover, really to know "the earth's eye," as Thoreau points out, you must sit on their surfaces and swim or fish in their depths. Eventually I placed crafts at both my ponds. I hid my little yellow canoe at Birch Pond and an old red rowing boat at Lilypad. Instantly my wild world widened. Now I can skim them easily any time of day, stalking spotted sandpipers and great blue herons, taking pictures, or just sunning.

How wealthy I was in ponds did not hit home until the fall of 1980. Storage space for my writing files is a constant problem at West of the Wind. I decided to dig beneath my log studio and enclose it as a small basement to increase room. Until then this waste area had been a porcupine motel. Every spring it was littered with rank droppings where the animals overwintered.

I hired a fine retired carpenter, Duke, to lay up the concrete blocks. I acted as his helper. One brisk afternoon he was mixing concrete and I was bringing him buckets of water, pails of sand, and bags of cement. One bag had been opened, a fact I did not notice until I plumped down the ninety-pound bag. The impact sent a blast of cement dust into my mouth, nostrils and eyes. Spitting, sputtering, blinking, I yelled for Duke. He told me to wash off the dust right away with water. I went indoors and splashed water from a bucket onto my face. At first I was unconcerned. Then my eyes started smarting. I splashed on more water; the pain increased. Duke came in with a fresh pail and ducked my whole head into the water. "Blink!" he ordered.

But the pain was so intense I could barely manage. The lids began swelling. "What does the bag say?" I cried.

"It says to wash skin or eyes thoroughly and seek medical attention," Duke read off. He grabbed my hand and pulled me toward the dock. "We'd better head down to the health center," he urged, "while you can still see. You may get worse, and you know I can't run an outboard, much less swim."

The clinic was twenty-five miles away by boat and truck. It became a feat of cooperation and endurance to get me there. I could no longer see. The pain was excruciating. This brave and intrepid man pulled the motor rope, got the engine started, and headed my boat in the right direction. I drove blindly, while Duke shouted orders.

"Jesus Christ—go left. You'll hit the shoals. Goddammit, you're heading straight for the shore. Straighten 'er out!"

We made it safely to the parking lot. Duke led me to the truck and pushed me into the cab. Condor jumped in the back. After driving rapidly to the health center, Duke parked and led me in, white with dust, streaked with tears and saliva, dressed in filthy work clothes. A doctor hurried in, examined me, then sat back with a grim expression.

"You've suffered severe chemical burns to your eyes," he said. "You should go by ambulance immediately to the nearest hospital for expert care."

Cold fear gripped my chest. I was terrified of being blind. Duke, wonderful friend that he was, immediately offered to drive me—truck, dog, and all. Bewildered, all I could think of, or wanted to do, was to have Mike in charge. But his hospital was a hundred miles away. Was time of critical importance?

"Yes!" said the local physician. Yet I knew no one in the closer city—no doctors, no friends. I'd been through a similar episode when I broke my pelvis and was carted off to a strange place. This time I might have to stay for days, or weeks, unable to see anything, alone.

"Wait!" I pleaded with the doctor as he began dialing to alert the strange hospital. "I don't want to go there. I want to go to my own physician's hospital. He'll find me a good ophthalmologist." I rattled off the name and number to call.

"That's too far," argued the G. P. "You need to—"

"I'll drive real fast," Duke interrupted. "It's only an hour farther. She'll feel better with folks she knows."

Perhaps Duke's firm stance and capable manner were convincing. The next thing I knew, drops of eye anesthetic were being squeezed onto my raw eyeballs, bringing temporary relief. Then Duke was dragging me out to the truck while the doctor placed the call. Mike's instruction was: "Get the hell down here fast as you can."

Duke stopped only three times on the way—for gas, for a bottle of whiskey for me, and for a clean shirt for him. As soon as the topical anesthetic wore off, the pain began in earnest. I was moaning throughout the trip. "Take a slug," Duke advised, "and put your head on my leg. I can still drive OK."

When we reached the hospital, Duke screeched to a halt near the emergency entrance. He quickly changed his shirt, then helped me out of the cab. Condor yelped frantically from the back. "Don't worry about your dog," Duke said soothingly. "I'll take him home with me."

I shuffled in, trying not to cry, holding Duke's arm, still clothed in my dirty rags. And then I heard a familiar, deep voice. "Here you are! What took so long? I'll take her, sir—and thank you. There's an eyeman waiting to check you out, Anne."

Two strong hands gripped my shoulders, squeezed them ever so slightly, and guided me toward an examining room. I could hear the crackle of a well-starched shirt and smell the aroma of after-shave lotion. "Sit down," Mike commanded. "Now look up at me." I stared blindly toward the ceiling.

Another person walked into the room, and I sensed rather than saw a bright beam of light directed onto my face. I heard a sharp intake of breath. Then hands gently opened my swollen lids. I cringed.

"I'm putting some special drops in to neutralize the caustic cement dust," explained a voice I didn't recognize. "It'll take several hours to counteract the burns and irritation on the inner lids, conjunctiva, and cornea. You'll have to stay here two or three days. Meanwhile, I'll give you a shot for pain."

"Thank God," I blubbered. "Please hurry." I felt near the breaking point.

"Will she see all right afterward?" Mike asked, getting right to the essentials.

"Yes. No permanent damage. Though she should avoid excessive eye use and strain for several days. She was lucky. When she ducked her head in that pail of water, she saved her eyes." I felt deep gratitude toward Duke.

"She'd have been better off to go jump in the lake," said Mike matter-of-factly.

Of course! The instant cure had been right under my nose, and I'd never thought of it. But part of my ignorance came from not knowing the dangerous properties of common cement. It's so much a part of the everyday world that I assumed it was harmless. How dumb could a woodswoman be?

Then there was the sharp sting of a needle in my upper arm, and a delicious drowsiness began closing. A wheelchair was brought in, and I was taken to be admitted. Mike walked companionably beside me. "Get some sleep," he said. "The nurses will wake you up every four hours for the next forty-eight to put in drops. I'll see you tomorrow."

In fact, when I did wake up next morning, Mike was coming briskly in the door. He was the first thing I saw in a blurry haze. My heart missed a beat. He looked like a vision to me.

I was hospitalized for three days, getting the caustic chemicals neutralized and washed out of my eyes. Woozy with pain-killers, I groped to dial numbers on a phone, fumbled for food with my fingers, and tripped going to the bathroom. I decided then and there that being blind would be the greatest disaster in life. Gradually my sight was restored.

As soon as I was discharged from the hospital, I hurried back to my cabin, stopping only to pick up Condor at Duke's house and leave him a gift. Seized with the desire to see the colors, sheens, and shadows of my Adirondack home, I raced up the lake in my boat. It was a still, clear autumn afternoon. I took a hammer, roofing nails, posted signs and a carpenter's apron, and set out to post my land. In one way it was a reaffirmation that I still belonged here; in another way it was an excuse to visit my ponds.

When I reached Lilypad, I stopped and sat down. Condor stretched out beside me. Tears started to run down my cheeks. *Everything was so beautiful.* Yet all of it had nearly been taken away from me forever. The fall foliage—burgundy, scarlet, crimson, and saffron—lay reflected on the water as in a mirror. Tawny grass on the shoreline shimmered in the slanting sun. Spires of green spruces lanced the brilliant sky. A lone jet trail slid silently toward the cleft in the hills, the only mark in the heavens. Back in the forest, a chipmunk went thunk-thunk-thunk. It was the only sound on this tremulous, golden, splendid day.

"What if I'd never seen this again?" I said out loud. "What if I'd never been able to walk to my ponds by myself?"

The thought was too demoralizing, for I knew the answer. Being blind would have meant leaving my cabin and moving to a city, where most of life is square, smooth, and level. Where the measure of predictability means that a blind person can achieve some degree of independence. Where you can gauge your steps to the supermarket, to a bus, to the laundry. But not here. Not in the Adirondacks, where roots and branches, waves and wind, crooked cabins and tippy canoes demand sight and coordination. The only thing that could have stayed constant in such a life would have been Condor. But he would have had to stop chasing squirrels and learn to be a Seeing Eye dog.

I had to smile at my own somber fantasy. I'd been spared, after all. I had been given more precious years to post my land, to visit my beloved ponds, and to *see* "the earth's eye."

6

Death from the Sky

As I sat on my dock at Black Bear Lake of an evening, watching the sunset, I seldom saw the boats of fishermen anymore. The trout were disappearing. I also noticed fewer and fewer ospreys and kingfishers patrolling the shallows. During the early years I had often swum near otters, for they used to sit on the rocks crunching trout dinners. Now they seemed scarcer. Those few that frolicked and fished here carried only bullheads, frogs, crayfish, or nothing at all. Moreover, during the past five or six summers the mighty chorus of bullfrogs that once boomed over the lake had diminished. Finally I counted only five bullfrogs at Black Bear Lake. There were none at all around Birch Pond, Lily-pad Lake, or Sunshine.

Loons, grebes, and herons have never nested here, to my knowledge, but usually one or two of these fish eaters fed or floated offshore in season. Lately they have been rare sights. Along with these water birds, the showy white water lilies on all three ponds have totally disappeared, although some cow lilies endure. Lilypad Lake is no longer a lily pad lake. My little lettuce garden down by the lakeshore no longer flourishes. I had to abandon it as the soil turned too acid. Mint and potatoes are about all that will grow.

At the same time that some plants and animals decreased, I could see that others throve. Water striders and boatmen were everywhere, and a green pondweed flourished. The bottom of Lilypad Lake became a solid, dense mat of sphagnum. Birch Pond was covered with a gray, feltlike carpet of filamentous algae.

Through all these subtle and not so subtle changes some things stayed the same. Blackflies prospered and fed on Condor and me each spring. Swallows continued to flit over the lakes, picking off water striders and blackflies. And spring peepers still trilled.

At first I merely puzzled over these changes with a personal but casual concern. Then, in 1978, *Outdoor Life* magazine asked me to write a story on a brand-new environmental problem—acid rain. Scientific awareness of acid rain in the United States had started in the mid-1970s, but the popular press and public had paid little attention. I began researching the problem. Everything I read confirmed what was happening at Black Bear Lake. Waters in the western Adirondacks and other mountain lakes were becoming acidified and damaged by a chemical fallout in the form of polluted air, rain, frost, snow, fog, dew, and even dust.

After writing my article, I turned my professional attention to the acid rain problem around my cabin. First I bought a portable pH meter to measure the acidity of water. Housed in a brief-case-size plastic box, it contained a probe to dip into water. This was connected to a meter which registered on a scale of from o to 14, or very acid to very alkaline. The box also held a bottle of distilled water to rinse the probe after each use and two nine-volt batteries.

During every rainstorm and sometimes in snowfalls I col-

Here I check an acid deposition station that monitors acid rain, snow, and dust twenty-four hours a day all year.

lected water samples and analyzed them. Compared to a neutral pH* of 7, or a so-called normal rain and snow of pH 5.7, my readings were way low. Local ponds and lakes averaged pH 4.5 in summer, 4.1 in late fall and early spring after the autumn rains and April thaw. An average Adirondack rain registered around 4.3. Once I got as low as 3.2. That is almost as acidic as vinegar!

By luck, I found a report giving pH readings from Black Bear Lake in 1933. Then the water was pH 6.3. That meant my lake was roughly *a hundred times* more acidic in 1983 as it had been fifty years earlier!

*pH means the power of hydrogen, or hydrogen ions present in solution.

Next, I started worrying about the otters and what their source of food would be now that fish life was disappearing. I examined their dried scats deposited on the rocks and found that they contained almost no fish bones or scales. Most were composed of small crayfish shells and frog skeletons. Presumably the otters were harvesting their food from deeper water and bottom mud. The acidity penetrated less there than at the surface. I stored the otter droppings in plastic containers (actually the Cool Whip ones used for my morning espresso) in order to assemble a record of otter food habit changes over the years.

As my anxiety about the Adirondack lakes grew, I started snorkeling to observe conditions underwater. Every time there was a heat wave, I would don my wet suit, mask, and flippers and check out a lake. The most dramatic was Brooktrout, way back in the West Canada Lakes Wilderness Area, lying at about twenty-two hundred feet. Long a traditional brook trout fishing lake, it lies five miles by trail from a dirt road, twelve miles more from a paved road, and another five from a town. Any conceivable source of pollution is more than thirty-five miles away.

I backpacked to Brooktrout with my gear and underwater camera and stayed overnight at the state lean-to. No night had ever seemed so still. From dusk to dawn, not a sound. Come morning, I scanned the shoreline with binoculars. No ripples broke the surface. There were no rising fish, stalking herons, swimming mergansers, or plopping frogs. Brooktrout had the eerie feeling of a cemetery.

Underwater I discovered an unnaturally clear blue world, reminiscent of the Bahamas. Visibility was excellent. I gazed down at submerged spruces, which had fallen years back, were still intact, yet now were a ghostly gray, covered with slimy algae. Nothing lived underwater here. Most of the zooplankton was gone, accounting for the clarity of the water. The fish that had given the lake its name were gone, too, along with the freshwater mussels, frogs, and crayfish. I snapped several underwater shots of this disturbing, surrealistic world.

Next, I dived in lakes that were still healthy, where acid rain had not had an impact. These were *large* lakes at *lower* elevations which had extensive watersheds with few rocks, thick soils, and well-forested shores. In direct contrast with Brooktrout Lake, their waters were brownish or greenish, alive with plankton. Visibility was limited to a few feet. Fish and amphibians moved about busily. White water lilies, cow lilies, pickerelweed, and other aquatic vegetation floated on the surface. Their long silvery stalks swayed gently in the waves, like beaded curtains in a doorway.

My underwater investigation clearly indicated that something was wrong with many high-elevation Adirondack lakes near my cabin. The New York State Department of Environmental Conservation claimed that close to six hundred lakes were threatened or "dead." And it appeared that more and more would be falling ill from the invisible "death from the sky" that was without taste, color, or smell.

In 1979, a year after my first article on acid rain, *National Geographic* approached me for another. The Adirondacks were fast becoming notorious as the "acid rain garbage dump" of our country as the result of air pollution on our prevailing winds, high elevations, thin, rocky soils, and heavy precipitation. Since I had lived in the area continuously, I could chronicle the environmental changes from personal experience.

I accepted the assignment from a sense of duty. My mountains and lakes were being hurt. Someone had to speak out and to as many people as possible. Eleven million people subscribe regularly to *National Geographic,* and an estimated twenty to twenty-five million read the magazine at doctors' and dentists' offices and in school libraries.

At the same time I was apprehensive. It would be the most

complicated piece I'd ever done, necessitating a working knowledge of chemistry, meteorology, geology, hydrology, physics, politics, biology, and more. The senior editor at *Geographic* encouraged me to attend conferences, interview scientists, and travel to other areas plagued by acid rain. Expenses were no problem. I had the backup of a marvelous photographer, Ted Spiegel, and two fine editors. Even so, the article took two years of research.

A trip to Scandinavia was essential. Its countries are harder hit by acidic deposition than the United States and Canada. Also, their scientists have been more deeply involved for a longer time in research than have North Americans. The "father of acid rain," Dr. Svante Odén, a soil scientist, is a Swede. With a stroke of genius he "discovered" the cause of this perplexing phenomenon in 1967. Over time, Dr. Odén reported an increasing pattern of acid deposition throughout much of Europe, including Scandinavia. He predicted many of the effects we see today. He compared acid rain to a "chemical warfare" among nations since such pollution honors no borders, no political powers.

Packing my pH meter, hiking boots, conference clothes, and a down parka, I headed for Scandinavia in October 1979. In Norway aquatic chemist Dr. Arne Henriksen guided me to a wild, rocky lake about three miles from the nearest road in the southern part of his country. "This is your classic acidified lake," he said. We arrived at midafternoon. The surface stretched mercury smooth, black as basalt, to a stony mountain backdrop. Gray cumulus clouds tinged with raspberry edged slowly overhead and were reflected in the still water. I listened. Not a sparrow sang. Not a cricket chirped. Not a squirrel chattered.

My colleague pulled a small rowboat from a shed and loaded it with scientific gear, food, and our camping stuff. Pulling away from shore, he dipped the probe of a pH meter into the lake. It read 4.3. Just like Black Bear and Brooktrout lakes!

"There are over sixty miles of green farms, forests, and fields from here to the sea," he said, gesturing south. "Then it's hundreds of miles over the ocean to the nearest sources of pollution in Great Britain and northern Europe. This acidity has to be blowing in long distances from *somewhere*!

"Our meteorological samples indicate that windborne dirty air emissions are coming from both places," he continued. "Scandinavia, especially southern Norway, is the long-range target; it's the same pattern as in your Adirondack Mountains that are dumped on by air pollution originating mainly in the midwestern United States, six hundred to eight hundred miles away."

We rowed to a rustic cabin under pines on a peninsula. Once it had been a private fishing lodge. Now it is a field station for acid rain research. A cold wind began sighing at sunset. Quickly we carried our gear inside and opened the heavy shutters of the cabin. Feeling right at home, I walked to the lake to fill buckets of water and out to the woodshed to tote in firewood. My companion laid a fire, using vertically stacked logs instead of horizontal ones. He touched a match to the kindling. Soon a ruddy glow was spreading over the hand-hewn log walls, where enormous brown trout trophies hung. Two were longer than my forearm with my fingers outstretched.

Pointing to the stuffed trout, Dr. Henriksen said, "Those fish were taken back in the 1930s. But not a fish has been caught here since 1945." He poured two small glasses of aquavit, pulled two chairs close to the hearth, and beckoned companionably to me. By now the fire was throwing its warmth out into the dank, cold room. We were able to stop moving around and sit down. Dr. Henriksen picked up a worn journal and thumbed through its yellowed pages. "Here it tells how the former owners tried restocking this lake several times. They introduced thousands of fish, yet none survived." His green eyes glinted in the firelight as he passed me the book. "In 1967 they suspected the problem might be acid rain. Finally, realizing their fishing lake was ruined, they offered the whole property to the Norwegian Acid Rain Project." He lapsed into silence and stared pensively into the flames.

It seemed so much like the sad situation at Black Bear Lake, except that in the States we were waking up ten years later. A strange feeling of déjà vu enveloped me. During our dinner a storm roared in, bringing rain. My colleague ran outside to collect a sample of water—pH 4.1. Later that night, as I lay on a rough-hewn bunk in my sleeping bag, I listened to the patter of rain-drops on the roof. It felt exactly like my cabin home. The four thousand miles between lakes disappeared. Acid rain is a very leveling agent.

In Sweden two even more impressive experiences gave me additional material for my article. One of the researchers I interviewed, Dr. Hans Hultberg, drove me through rural lands west of Göteborg. We bounced over rough roads, stopping frequently at tidy farmsteads that looked perfectly normal.

"You see that place over there?" The scientist pointed. "The babies had diarrhea off and on for months until we found that their well water was very acid and was leaching copper from the plumbing lines. This caused a high content of this heavy metal in the drinking water, hence into the food and milk of the babies. Once they were switched to pure bottled water, their diarrhea stopped."

Farther on we passed a small cottage and garden. "The lady who lives there," explained my colleague, "used to wash her hair in well water. As you see, most of us Swedes are blond, but *her* hair was *green*—tinted green by the copper sulfate leached into her well by acid rain. Green as a birch in spring!"

At still another homestead he described the owner as a kidney patient on dialysis. "This man is forced every week, to travel a long way to a large hospital, where the water is highly filtered and distilled. If he tried to use the water at his home, he would be toxified. It is full of aluminum leached out of the soil by acid deposition."

At the end of our day Dr. Hultberg summarized by saying that the effects of acid rain itself will seem minor when compared to the toll of heavy metals and aluminum accumulation in the future.

The high point of my investigation was a sailing trip on the Baltic Sea with Dr. Odén. At first I was perplexed why he wanted to go *there* for evidence of acid deposition since salt water neutralizes the sulfuric and nitric acids in acid precipitation. Yet he assured me that an interesting experiment lay ahead.

That October day was one of hammered gold and royal blue —a true Swedish fall day. The Baltic churned and flashed under a chilly wind. Suddenly it didn't much matter *what* we discovered. I had never seen such magical slanting light or been so far north before. We stashed a picnic in the galley and hoisted the sails. Then the small boat heeled over, and we were prancing toward low, rocky islands off to starboard.

The robust scientist stood at the helm, his blue eyes squinted into slits from the spray and sun, giving his face the look of a Lapp. He wore a pair of high rubber boots and a huge hand-knit white fisherman's sweater. His blond hair was tousled above a weather-beaten, tanned face. I felt as if a Viking had spirited me away.

We came into the lee of a point, and he dropped anchor close to shore. After jumping onto shore, he produced a pH meter and dipped its probe into the sea—pH 7.5, which is normal. Then he walked backward, stopping at tiny pools of rainwater left from the last storm and caught in clefts between rocks. The first read pH 6.5. It was about ten feet from shore and obviously subjected to salt spray from the waves. The second lay twenty-five feet from shore and read 5.5. The last, a good seventy-five feet away from the sea and its influence, was 4.5. Acid rain! It was a simple yet brilliant demonstration.

Beckoning me to follow, Dr. Odén walked toward some shrubby growth. "I've been sailing around these islands for several summers," he explained, "and have watched these plants sicken. Mark my words, the future of forests is at stake. After the lakes and fish go, after the soils are stripped of nutrients and trace metals, then the trees will start to die. It just takes them longer to respond to the poisoning than trout or salamanders."

The overall impact of these experiences was so strong that I decided to attend a high-level meeting on long-range transport of air pollution at the United Nations in Switzerland. I was anxious to hear what plans were being made to control emissions in Europe and compare them to U.S. strategies.

In the elegant halls of the UN the heads of environmental

Dr. Sante Oden, "father of acid rain," on his boat in Sweden.

agencies and air pollution divisions from thirty-one of the 33 European nations were present. Sadly I listened to heart-rending appeals by the Norwegian and Swedish delegates to stop the pollution devastating their countrysides. Then, in astonishment, I heard expert testimony from the United Kingdom to the effect that there was *no* scientific evidence to link smoke from English electrical generating plants to fish and forest damage in Scandinavia. I was even more outraged to listen as West German officials refused to initiate emission controls on their steel plants and other factories because of the cost involved and insufficient evidence of damage then.

In simplest terms, certain upwind countries were dumping their pollution onto downwind countries and either neglecting to —or refusing to—clean up their mess. The Scandinavian situation bore a strong analogy to the Adirondack one. Yet, nation or state, it is *ethically* no different from a neighbor at Black Bear Lake flinging his garbage onto my land and turning his back, rather than driving to the dump, burning, or burying it.

I returned home with a far greater understanding of the political and sociological forces at work in the acid rain arena—and with an appreciation of those Scandinavians I met. It was apparent to me that they were far more attuned to environmental health and nature than most Americans. The Swedes and Norwegians were sincerely trying to mitigate the acid rain problem. I did not sense there, as in America, a persistent paranoia about finances, political stances, and legalities. It seemed to me that Scandinavians believe the poisoning of their countryside is *wrong* and should be stopped. Solutions did not depend wholly on the monetary losses to fishing or tourism, the costs of scrubbers, or the extra dollars that citizens might have to pay to clean up air pollution.

Moreover, the Scandinavians were not stalling cleanup actions by conducting more and more research, as our country has been doing. They were putting efforts into cleaning up their *own* mess, even though they are the victims. Of the acid deposition in Norway and Sweden 80 percent is "imported" from other European nations, whereas, only 20 percent originates "at home." Already eighteen thousand of the eighty-five thousand Swedish lakes, plus many of the great Norwegian fishing rivers, have been affected in some degree by acid rain. Yet the Scandinavians have already eliminated 30 to 60 percent of their own dirty air.

At this writing it has been five years since publication of my *National Geographic* article. It seems to me the Adirondacks are in worse shape than before. I know of three scary things that have been happening right in my backyard. My old guide friend Rodney has had to replace the entire plumbing system of his house. The stout copper lines installed fifty years ago lasted for about thirty-five years. He replaced them. But in fewer than fifteen years the new lines pitted and corroded through. They are full of pinpricks where aggressive acidic water etched away the metal. Other neighbors are complaining of the same problem and expense.

Then an environmental health scientist from the New York State Department of Health sampled the groundwater of several Adirondack domestic wells and springs not long ago. I helped guide him to these locations, some of them back in the woods beyond human habitation. As in western Sweden, surprisingly high levels of aluminum and mercury showed up in springwater (leached by acid rain from the soils), and copper and lead in plumbing systems (leached from the lines). The scientist strongly urged that water which has lain overnight in metal (not plastic) plumbing systems be flushed out by running the tap for two or three minutes before mixing frozen orange juice or making coffee.

Finally, right around my cabin there used to be sixteen enormous virgin red spruce trees. They were the ones that I worried would fall on my roof during windstorms and crush me in the sleeping loft. Of these sixteen, four have fallen harmlessly to high winds. The others started turning a peculiar yellow-green color and losing needles at the crowns. For several years they bore an extra-heavy crop of cones. Then all the foliage gradually dropped off. Only three trees are still alive. Many have snapped in two. When I pick up the shards of wood, they are as dry and brittle as papier-mâché. Useless!

To make sure this wasn't just an odd occurrence in the vicinity of my cabin, I paddled around the shoreline of Black Bear Lake, counting dead and live spruces. The results? Thirty-five percent of the big trees were dead or dying.

The same phenomenon is taking place on the upper slopes (at elevations of twenty-five to thirty-five hundred feet) of the High Peaks in the Adirondacks. An estimated 60 to 90 percent of the spruces are dead or in severe decline.

An even more extensive forest dieback has taken place in West Germany and several other European countries in the past decade. About five years ago West Germany reported a 34 percent reduction of firs, pines, spruces, and beeches in its mountainous areas. Today the die-off has affected 54 percent of these trees. Millions of acres of woodland are partially dead. The phenomenon is called *Waldsterben*, "forest death." Poland, East Germany, Czechoslovakia, along with Sweden, Norway, and the Netherlands, are reporting a similar tragedy.

Scientists strongly suspect that the culprit is acid deposition, acting in concert with certain weather and soil conditions. Acidic water leaches trace elements from soils, inducing nutrient loss and stress. Slowly the trees begin to starve and sicken. Acidic water also releases aluminum and heavy metals that kill fine root hairs. Slowly the trees die of thirst.

To combat *Waldsterben*, stringent air pollution controls be-

---

Research teams from the Department of Environmental Conservation come by helicopter to monitor acidity at many Adirondack lakes.

gan going into effect during 1986 in West Germany to cut emissions of sulfur dioxide and nitrous oxides from new power plants, vehicles, and factories. Older facilities will undergo abatement procedures of various kinds. The use of unleaded gas and lower speed limits on the autobahns are also being planned. West Germany has pledged a 33 percent reduction, or more, of these acid rain precursors by 1993. By contrast no Eastern European country appears to be addressing the problem.

I suppose I can console myself that in the space of five years I have had the bitter satisfaction of seeing the West German government do a complete about-face in its position toward acid rain and international pollution. After years of exporting vast quantities of unclean air to downwind nations (at least 50 percent of Sweden's acidic deposition comes from this highly industrialized nation) and believing itself immune to the problem, West Germany has bowed to the inevitable.

Political solutions clearly *are* possible. And Mother Nature may still repair the biological damage before it's irreversible. Unfortunately that is not the case in our country. Our federal government is no closer to reauthorizing, amending, and strengthening the Clean Air Act as of this writing than it was in 1980. It appears that each state may have to act if any cleanup is to happen. Already New York and a couple others have.

Meanwhile, I walk my woods and paddle my ponds, fingers to the pulse points, diagnosing, evaluating. It feels a little like watching a lover or a dear friend die a lingering death. Each year my woods and ponds seem a little worse, a little more anemic, a bit more toxified. I hope against hope that a remission is still possible. Yet I believe that the only effective therapy is to reduce sulfur dioxide and nitrous oxide emissions (with the accompanying toxic metals) and ozone by about 70 to 80 percent.

No one asked my permission to kill trout and spruces. I, and they, are innocent victims. I worry. Is our bracing mountain air bad for our lungs? Is drinking lake water of pH 4.3 by the bucketful injurious to our intestines? Or brushing teeth with springwater twice a day eroding enamel? How about swimming every dawn? Will we humans, like trees, take a long time to respond to the effects of an acidified environment?

There's no way to escape those acid-bearing storm clouds that push over the mountains. It has taken fifty years to degrade my environment to its present state; it will probably take fifty years to recuperate. So even if laws were passed tomorrow, and the mechanical cleanups begun, a healthy Adirondacks would be decades away.

Imagine how many times the earth must turn until the showy white water lilies, the giant red spruces, the booming bullfrogs, and the native brook trout come back again to my woods and ponds. I've come to realize, with a pang, that I won't live to see them return.

7

The Decision
to Retreat

W *Acid Rain* is not all that upsets me. When I purchased my
property, Black Bear Lake was peaceful and unpopulated.
Over the years I've seen extraordinary environmental and sociological changes take place. Dumb me—I naïvely thought my little
"paradise" would stay pristine and serene forever.

Naturally some changes and improvements were to be expected. The summer population had gradually increased from one
permanent retired couple and roughly twenty summer cottage
dwellers to two retired men and sixty summer camp folk. Families
were expanding. They needed vacation space for their offspring.
Then the children were marrying, having babies, and seeking to
expand even more. Boathouses were converted into camps, and
guest cottages squeezed onto existing properties. As roads, boats,
motors, and vehicles improved, more people came more often to
the lake and stayed longer.

Not surprisingly, most summer people wanted greater conveniences. Older folks worried about heart attacks; younger ones, about accidents to the kids. First, they petitioned for a power line around the lake; then, for an underwater phone cable. Finally, a garbage Dumpster was installed at the public parking lot. A lot more garbage was and is being generated these days, and it is no longer being thrown onto the traditional trash heaps behind camps back in the woods. So our backlots are tidier than before, yet after long holiday weekends I cringe to see these bins overflowing with garbage bags, empty beer cartons, discarded bedsprings, and used paint cans.

As more people used Black Bear Lake, a suspicion arose about our collective sewage. Were everyone's leach fields, septic tanks, and plumbing adequate and intact? Or was the lake in which many of us swam, sailed, and canoed and from which we drank the water gradually being polluted?

I brought up this touchy subject at a property owners' meeting. It was decided we should make a survey. At that time private citizens had no authority to check camps or force a cleanup. All we could do was order a box of septic tank dye and ask neighbors voluntarily to put a scoop in their toilets. When flushed down the drain, the dye would show up any leaks in the septic system by seeping out as a startling fluorescent chartreuse color in the lake.

Eventually we were able to hire a pollution officer from the township to check various camps. Since there is no road around Black Bear Lake, he had to be transported from cottage to cottage. I volunteered my boat and time for the task. In order to remain as neutral and anonymous as possible, I merely dropped the officer at various docks and stayed in my boat reading or writing. It took him about thirty minutes per camp.

In his survey of some twenty-five vacation homes that summer he found three offenses. One camp was running kitchen water (gray water) right onto the ground with a hose so that the fats, soapy suds, and table tidbits lay exposed. These could be washed into the lake after a heavy rain. At another the officer discovered a cracked section of pipe right under a boathouse toilet. Frost had heaved it. As a result, raw sewage was dribbling directly into the lake. The third infraction was a dry well dug too close to shore, uncovered, and no leach field. At all three sites the pollution officer wrote out citations. The residents had thirty days to comply with the public health law and correct their problems.

In each case it took money to change the violations. Some people had limited funds or didn't feel like spending what they had on a seldom-used second home at Black Bear Lake. Selfishly all they cared about was saving dollars rather than the overall health and safety of our community lake. Yet if just one case of typhoid, *Giardia*, or hepatitis had ever shown up here, everyone would be at peril.

One night I returned to Black Bear Lake at midnight after attending a local meeting. There was no moon, and the sky was overcast. Moving mostly by touch, I pushed my boat into the water and yanked at the outboard motor rope. Nothing happened. I yanked again and again. The smell of gas was overpowering. I got a spotlight from my truck and ran its beam over the engine. Everything seemed in order. I knew the spark plugs were fresh and the tank was full. I reached down to squeeze the bulb, and gas spurted all over my legs. The gas line had been cut in two! One short section was still attached to the tank; another, to the motor. But the middle piece was lying onshore, where it had been thrown.

Clearly someone was trying to tell me something. I guessed I was being blamed for ferrying the pollution officer around the lake. Perhaps a camp owner was incensed at being forced to conform to the health ordinances. Suspiciously I mentally reviewed each of the violators. Was one of them responsible? In Adirondack society a cut gas line to a boat engine is equivalent to sugar dropped into the gas tank of a car. In both cases, human life could be jeopardized by a nonfunctioning vehicle.

Furious, I retrieved the sections of rubber hose and carefully put them in a plastic bag. I hoped there might be fingerprints on them. I jumped in my boat, set my oars in the locks, and rowed briskly home. I was too angry to sleep.

The next day I called the state police and reported the incident. They came to Black Bear Lake to investigate but never found the culprit. To this day, whenever I leave my boat at the parking lot, I remove the gas hose and chain the tank to the gunwales.

As for outboard motors, they have proliferated at my lake—both in number and horsepower size. It used to be that people depended on canoes and guide boats for transportation up and down the two-mile body of water. Then gas-driven motorboats took over. Today only one or two families rely steadfastly on the old muscle-powered method. Everyone else whizzes around with engines—many large enough to water-ski behind—even a hundred-horse Mercury! I maintain that our lake should be limited to motors of fifteen horsepower or less—or none at all—and that each and every Adirondack lake be assigned its own carrying capacity for outboard motorboats. The smaller the lake, the smaller the motor. Otherwise we run the risk of becoming like Lake George with its estimated ten thousand boats on a busy summer weekend, roaring, smoking, sideswiping, and endangering swimmers and canoeists.

On busy summer holidays there are times when the lake is abuzz with gas engines—chain saws, ATVs, pumps, lawn mowers, Rototillers, floatplanes—breaking the silence that once stretched from hill to hill. The bigger motorboats throw up wakes which erode the shoreline and rock our docks constantly. When the traffic is fierce, the two rocking chairs on my dock look as if they were nodding and chatting over a private conversation all day.

In defense I go camping on Memorial Day, the Fourth of

One of Condor's first backpacking trips with me.

July, and Labor Day. I can't bear to sit in my cabin and listen to what's happening. Enginemania. So Condor and I choose a place in a wilderness area where motorized intrusions are prohibited. In the Adirondacks there are sixteen such tracts, totaling 1,050,000 acres or 20 percent of all designated state and federal wilderness east of the Rocky Mountains and 85 percent of the designated wilderness in the eleven northeastern states. Thank heaven such places still exist, for in the eastern United States sound pollution has infiltrated to an astonishing degree. It may be contributing to hearing loss, stress, high blood pressure, and cardiac problems.

Even when I am camping, there's one form of noise I cannot escape. That comes from the fighter planes which practice war games above the Adirondacks. Originating from air bases near Rome, Plattsburgh, and Syracuse, New York, the planes use our mountains to train in radar detection avoidance because these areas are so "sparsely settled"—as if 120,000 permanent residents did not count. More to the point, they often zoom down over Black Bear Lake as a "target of opportunity."

Once I was painting my roof, perched precariously on a ladder, when two fighter jets abruptly roared a hundred feet above the ridgepole. They sounded as if they were breaking the sound barrier! I practically plummeted to the ground. Several times I've been sunbathing by the lake when a jet reconnaissance plane suddenly swooped low over the water, right above my dock, supposedly taking evasive action from a chase plane. The nerve-ripping whine reverberated from shore to shore. Tears always spring to my eyes as I imagine the lethal cargo such planes can unload on unsuspecting people (and did unleash in Vietnam).

An even more frightening incident occurred one Saturday morning at the height of summer. A Cessna seaplane landed on Black Bear Lake to take weekenders up for a scenic flight. I saw the plane taxi and take off into the wind. Hard at work writing on my sun deck, I paid no more attention. Half an hour later, at 11:00 A.M., the faint drone of the returning floatplane could be heard behind the mountain at the head of the lake.

A moment later two A-10 fighter jets approached the lake at right angles. Suddenly their usual roar escalated to an earsplitting whine as they screeched skyward right above my cabin. Like a starburst, they clawed for altitude to avoid collision with the incoming seaplane. Seconds later the floatplane landed safely on Black Bear Lake.

My heart leaped into my throat as I realized the close call we'd all had. Not only would an air collision have killed the two highly skilled jet pilots and destroyed their multimillion-dollar planes, but it would have wasted the seaplane, the bush pilot, and his passengers. Morever, the force of the explosion might have damaged camps and injured boaters with flying debris. Needless to say, the publicity would have been scandalous.

When I talked to the passengers of the floatplane later, they stated that the A-10s had lifted almost vertically in front of their eyes, and the floatplane then passed *between* their jet trails! Either one of those jet wakes conceivably could have given the little seaplane a tossing from its turbulence.

All in all, the maneuvering of these training jets was rarely hazardous but always annoying to us camp owners and visitors on the ground. No one wanted to see smashed planes and dead pilots in our woods and on the lake. Everyone hated the sudden noise. In addition, their flights above wilderness areas might be frightening certain birds and mammals.

Nevertheless, it is in America's national defense interests that the Air National Guard pilots practice their "nap of the earth" (close to the ground) radar detection training. This form of sound pollution will not stop. However, I began wondering if the A-10s could be rerouted away from wilderness areas, Black Bear Lake, and their apparent zeroing in on my dock and my belly button.

As if power lines, noise, big boats, telephones, jets, and Dumpsters are not enough, there is also the specter of pesticides in the private lands of the Adirondack Park. After years of streams being treated with DDT blocks to kill blackfly larvae, the well-known ecological derangement documented in Rachel Carson's *Silent Spring* occurred here. Bald and golden eagles, peregrine falcons, and ospreys were contaminated and laid thin-shelled eggs. Most cracked under the weight of incubating parents or failed to hold viable young or living chicks. These birds of prey almost disappeared from the Adirondacks, as they did elsewhere. DDT was banned.

Aerial spraying with chemical pesticides replaced DDT as a

blackfly control technique. Stuff like chlordane, Dibrom, and me-thoxychlor was spread by small planes and road foggers every spring over populated places. Fortunately state law does *not* allow spraying on state lands (i.e., the forest preserve), so 2.4 million acres are spared. It is the private lands that are targeted.

Recognizing the threat to small birds, fish, amphibians, and drinking water, our property owners' group agreed to prohibit the aerial spraying of these toxic chemicals around Black Bear Lake. We sent an appropriate letter to the township's officials. They complied, but not without comment, I might add. Even today the village people of Lake Serene mutter, "Crazy folk up at Black Bear Lake. They must love being eaten alive."

Yet nothing I've experienced indicates that spraying has long-lasting effects on blackflies. Unless you're playing golf right after the spray plane goes over or are sitting on your front lawn getting doused by a fogger truck, the pesky critters come back to bite you a few minutes or hours later. Since we've stopped spraying at Black Bear Lake, I've not noticed any appreciable increase in the number of bites or severity of attacks year after year. In fact, I sit typing on my sundeck all spring, between the hours of 10:00 A.M. to 3:00 P.M., when the hot sun and lake breeze discourage flies. Those evenings when humidity makes them bite, I just start a smudge fire and dab on Ole Time Woodsman's repellent. It seems to me that songbirds and dragonflies do a better job of making blackflies disappear than spray planes and town officials.

Along with the sickening knowledge that I'll never see my woods and waters regain ecological health as the result of acid rain, and that my woodland world was being invaded and my time fragmented, I came to realize I could not escape these other forms of technology at Black Bear Lake. Unless I sold out and moved to New Zealand, Alaska, the Amazon basin, or Iceland, I was stuck with these changes around my cabin. All I could do was fight small holding actions, like controlling sewage and banning spraying. Not an easy conclusion for a woodswoman and ecologist to have to come to.

Yet I thought there had to be some small consolation, some compromise. I'm not sure how the idea came to me. Perhaps it was triggered by still *one more* uninvited visitor, or an especially loud sonic boom, or an extra big wake crashing on my dock. Or all of them . . . No matter. One day, after years of vacillating, I simply decided to retreat beyond Black Bear Lake. To find a tiny bit of privacy and peace. To go deeper into the forest where days and nights would become whole again. I had taken all I could of intrusions, whether they were strangers appearing in the night, crank calls, piles of fan mail, big boats, gas motors, people, planes, and pollution. In short, I was fed up with the public world.

The one place I could think of and wanted to go to was Lily-pad Lake. My long-ago dream of having a tiny cabin way back there flowered afresh. The land was free. Part belonged to me; the rest to the state of New York. It was uninhabited and beautiful. The lake was close enough to my cabin to be practical, even though no roads or trails, power, or phones existed. My mind began busying itself with the logistics of transportation and construction. My soul envisioned the excitement of pioneering a new homestead, then undisturbed days of writing, reading, and walking. After all, how many people have the chance to re-create a backwoods haven in the twentieth century in the northeastern United States? To become a latter-day Thoreau? Actually to live like Thoreau? Like him, I felt my purpose in going to Lilypad Lake was "to transact some private business with the fewest obstacles" and "to front only the essential facts of life."

Three things were certain. Considering the distance, hilly topography, lack of routes, and personal economics, my new cabin must be constructed from logs cut at the site. The very minimum of store-bought materials would be utilized, and only equipment and furnishings that could be backpacked. The heaviest item—a wood stove—would have to be dragged up by toboggan in winter, when snow made the going easier. Lastly, I decided to spend as little money as possible on the entire cabin. Rereading *Walden*, I found Thoreau had paid $28.12 1/2 for *his* ten-by-fifteen-foot house, plus $2.00 for oil and some household items, or $30.12 1/2. He figured he had built a lifetime shelter at an expense no greater than a student pays for his *annual* rent. By today's standards (140 years later), a student might pay ten times this amount for one *month!* Anyway, I resolved to build and furnish *my* shelter for around $300. Or ten times more.

The most immediate requirement was to scout out a route which was as level as possible. There was my little yellow canoe at Birch Pond. It might be feasible to use it as an intermediate link of transportation. By paddling up Birch, I could save a quarter of a mile of walking and toting. So I brushed out a narrow trail from my cabin to the pond and put my canoe at the trailhead. Then I scouted another route connecting the upper part of the pond with Lilypad Lake. The two small knolls made the going somewhat arduous. Part of the way followed old deer trails and ancient fishing paths. Then I walked and paddled the whole route through. It took perhaps forty-five minutes. Perfect for privacy. Longfellow's lines about Hiawatha's canoe danced in my head:

> Like a yellow leaf in autumn,
> Like a yellow waterlily.

Routing done, I was ready to begin building Thoreau II.

8

Big Brother Is
Watching

My first load up to Thoreau II the summer of 1984 consisted of an ax, a small saw, a pry bar, and a tape measure. My first job was to clear and measure off a site for the new cabin. I planned to use the same spot where my makeshift lean-to and log shelter had stood. Several years of growth, however, had sprung up while I'd been busy working and traveling. This neglect had caused the sills to rot and the floor to crumble. Young balsams sprouted vigorously inside and around the foundation. I began cutting them down and dragging them away. That done, I threw out the old sodden logs.

Next, I found a little swale and started prying rocks out for fresh foundation posts. Because of the cold Adirondack winters and wet summers, buildings cannot be set directly on the ground or they will frost heave and decay. Rock digging was rough work. Soon I was covered with mud and scratches. The blackflies kept me company, adding to the general mess with bloody bites and trickles. Nevertheless, I was reveling in this labor when an unsettling thought struck me—the Adirondack Park Agency! This state land use planning agency had mandated certain rules and regulations for every acre of private land in the park. Could it be that my proposed retreat would possibly need a permit?

I sat down abruptly, scratching behind my ears at bites. My mind raced over the agency regulations, in force since 1973. As well as I could recall, the type of zoning around Black Bear Lake on private land was "rural use." It called for a building lot to be set back 75 feet from the mean high water of the shoreline; for septic systems to be 100 feet from any water body; and for a lot to have a lakeshore width of 150 feet. I had already planned on these setbacks and had 500 feet of shoreline. So, I reasoned, Thoreau II conformed in all respects. Besides, why should this austere agency, which dealt with critical issues like the ninety- and seventy-meter ski jumps for the 1980 Olympics, huge subdivisions, state prisons, hotel and condo developments, be concerned about a tiny structure without utilities, without a road, and so far from anything? It could care less.

I got up and went blithely back to rock digging and hauling. When there were enough stones, I dug four holes down to hardpan, making a square about twelve by twelve feet. These were filled with rocks until they formed piles a foot above the ground. This phase of the cabin took a few afternoons and, of course, cost absolutely nothing.

The second phase of construction was to begin cutting straight spruce trees on my land and hauling them to the site. With a floor space of twelve by twelve feet, I would need logs fourteen to sixteen feet long, with diameters of four to six inches. Yet a green log that size is a little too much heft and weight for a woman five feet four inches and 120 pounds. I could easily cut and trim the trees, but after that I needed either a skidding horse or a strong friend to help haul the logs. Sad to say, the former is a thing of the past; the latter, thankfully, is still in good supply. Everyone I invited up to help that summer seemed excited at the prospect of building a wilderness cabin. Like pioneers, we dragged the logs with large hooked ice tongs through the forest over irksome roots and through dense tangles. Gradually my pile of logs grew.

Not wishing to mar the scenery or change the forest composition, I cut only the four big base logs near the site. For the rest, I cruised my timber carefully, picking specimens as far away as an eighth of a mile. It took extra time and energy to haul them so far, but the woods were left looking almost untouched.

When the July meeting of the Adirondack Park Agency rolled around, I prudently decided to ask one of our lawyers his opinion of my project. I had sat as a commissioner on the agency for eight years and was proud of it. Moreover, I espoused most of its environmental laws. It would not do to goof up personally after all this time. In younger days, I would have gone ahead in a happy-go-lucky way, but I remembered only too vividly the mess with West of the Wind. I'd foolishly neglected to read the deed when I bought my land and built my cabin. A covenant therein stated that any building must be fifty feet back from the lakeshore. Innocently I had constructed the cabin thirty-eight feet from the lake. My reason was to avoid cutting any virgin red spruces or white pines and to take advantage of a small rise for a tranquil view down Black Bear Lake.

A shiver of despair still runs down my back when I recall the specter of an irate lawyer, well into his cups, it seemed, bearing down on me, thundering, "You've broken your deed! You're too close to the lake! I'll take you to court unless you remove that offending structure!"

His dire proclamation, coming on the heels of a recent divorce and my father's death, had really rocked me. With the help of wonderful friends, I'd finally moved the cabin—all fourteen tons of wood and metal roof—inch by laborious inch, twelve and a half feet. We used jacks, come-alongs, and greased logs. Then the cabin stood a legal and respectable fifty and a half feet from the shoreline. But, by abiding to the letter of the law, I was forced to cut five huge spruce trees, gouge up the land, and perch my little home like a long-legged wading bird on posts beside a damp depression. Before, it had scarcely been noticeable from a boat; now it was visible from the lake. I certainly didn't need a repeat of *that* performance.

I described my project in detail to our APA attorney, just in case I was missing something in the lawbooks. To my discomfort, he gave me a guarded answer. "I *think* you're OK without a permit, but I want to check our regs and maps more closely." I went home with the nagging feeling that all was not well.

A week later I received a crisp legal letter informing me that a permanent building of the size I proposed required a permit under agency statutes because it would lie within an eighth of a mile of a wilderness area!

I was stunned. "Big Brother" had struck again. The very things I wished to escape from—bureaucracy, intrusions, disturbances, red tape—were once more fouling up my life. Bitterly I recalled Thoreau saying, "Wherever a man goes, men will pursue and paw him with their dirty institutions, and, if they can, constrain him. . . . I was never molested by any person but those who represented the state."

Feeling as if I were jousting with the devil, I then wrote back to the APA to see if Thoreau II might be nonjurisdictional considering that I'd had a lean-to and cabin frame there *prior* to the new agency's laws. I knew the rules were for the good of everyone in the park, yet I could not bear seeing my dream retreat thwarted.

After what seemed like an interminable period, during which time I was afraid to cut any more logs, a typed, single-spaced, three-page letter came back. It stated that the eight-of-a-mile portion of land where Thoreau II was supposed to stand was a "critical environmental area." In order to build the cabin and *not* need a permit, the cabin could not exceed *a hundred square feet in size.* Essentially it had to constitute a "renovation and improvement" of my old structure and must be akin to a hunting and fishing cabin in design. Furthermore, the letter went on, it could be used by me only for *occasional* occupancy as a "retreat." In this way Thoreau II could become an accessory structure to West of the Wind, thus exempt from agency review.

The letter went on to explain that the "rural use" restrictions on sewage disposal and lot width also applied. Furthermore, there was the matter of certain vegetation-cutting restrictions. To quote: "Within 35 feet of the mean high water mark, not more than 30% of the trees in excess of a diameter breast height of six inches existing at any time could be cut over any ten-year period. And within six feet of this mark, no vegetation could be removed, except that up to a maximum of 30% of the shorefront could be cleared of vegetation on any individual lot."

When I finished reading all this, my head was reeling. What irony! As a commissioner who dealt monthly with the applications, permits, variances, approvals, and denials of *other* people's projects, I was now being told what and how to conduct *my* business. This made me froth at the mouth, even as I knew these environmental and developmental controls were basically for the good of the Adirondacks. What a dilemma!

It was a humbling experience and a valuable one. It put me closer in touch with our 120,000 permanent park residents than ever before. It made me question some of these state laws, how bewildering they can be and how—at times—unbalanced. I'll always chafe at the knowledge that our mountains and lakes are now harnessed by regulations. One can no longer just head into the woods and homestead. Zoning is becoming a way of life as world populations press harder and harder on resources and land space. Yet in some small corner of my soul it still rankles that I *have* to conform. I love personal freedom, and I guess I believe that in all the Adirondacks hardly anyone has as great a sensitivity, aesthetically and ecologically, for our mountain country as I do. Or as large a love.

Be that as it may, without a "big brother" watching over the Adirondacks and its backcountry areas, anyone could throw up a marina or a hot dog stand beside a wild lake, put in a condo or retirement village atop a forested mountain. Such developments certainly do belong in the park, but only in carefully designated

As a board member of the Adirondack Park Agency, I often make aerial reconnaissance of the park in a Department of Environmental Conservation helicopter.

places like hamlets, towns, high-intensity-use areas, camp and ski grounds. They do *not* belong at the edge of wilderness areas or marring magnificent scenery. Truly they are "critical environmental areas" which deserve protection.

When all my feathers had smoothed down, I figured nothing much had really happened. I had never planned to live full-time at Thoreau II anyway. A hundred-square-foot cabin was just a little smaller than what I'd started with at West of the Wind. I could accommodate. After all, "small is beautiful." I'd never planned to cut the shoreline vegetation other than some fastidious trimming to frame the view across Lilypad Lake. Thoreau II would definitely always look like a hunting and fishing cabin, even though acid rain and overuse had made inroads. Thoreau II was simply to be a retreat.

Anyway, I was now free and clear to go ahead with my dream. Once again the pile of logs swelled. After my pals and I had cut about forty-five logs for walls, six log rafters, and assorted posts, we stopped. I drew some sketches on scrap paper of the way the tiny cabin should look—one big window facing the lake, a tiny garret, a door to the south, and a trapper's type of slant roof. I was ready to begin.

9

Half a Haven

W *The delay in construction* at Thoreau II brought three advantages. The bugs were gone, the days were cooler, and I was brimming with impatience. If possible, I wanted to finish the cabin before early snows fell and I had to leave on winter's work. Therefore, in order to move things ahead more swiftly, I started organizing "pioneer work parties" each weekend in late summer.

The first friends who came to help were a family from a big farm in western New York. They were used to hard work, loved to camp, and adored Condor. The father, Karl, was a longtime acquaintance, and his two children, Ricky and Linda, had read my "Ranger Rick" articles and children's books over the years. We planned to camp in my lean-to near West of the Wind and walk back and forth daily to Lilypad Lake.

Our plan was to cut down and drag in more building logs and to complete the floor of the tiny cabin. Before we could begin, however, a mountain of equipment had to be backpacked up to Lilypad Lake. This included two chain saws, gas and oil, axes, carpenter tools, food and water, a first-aid kit, ear protectors, nails and spikes, twelve sheets of particle board, and cookies for Condor. I wondered about Ricky and Linda. Though they were energetic and wiry, both were small and could manage only limited loads. The quarter-inch particle sheets (I planned to double them for strength) were far too heavy and bulky for the youngsters to carry. So Karl and I manhandled the four-by-eight-foot boards through the woods to my yellow canoe on Birch Pond, while the kids lugged all the other gear in their packs.

I had to chuckle at the sight of them. Linda, quite the young woman at fifteen, was wearing lipstick and nail polish, but within the hour her mouth was smudged, her nails were chipped, and her red hair was in flaming disarray. Yet she kept gamely to the task. Ricky, in contrast, looked like a regular Huck Finn, full of freckles and with a thatch of dark, unruly hair. He carried a big hunting knife in his belt and wore enormous boots.

Every trip to the cabin site had to count. Therefore, we piled the twelve sheets of particle board atop the canoe gunwales. The small craft sank gradually to within two inches of its edges. There was barely room for Ricky and me to perch and paddle. Just as we pushed off from shore, Condor dashed out of the woods and leaped upon our cargo. By some miracle, he landed dead center on the boards. The canoe didn't capsize. Condor sat down and surveyed the scenery. Obviously there was no way to discourage him from accompanying us on this trip. So off we went like some gigantic dragonfly with its wings spread and a seventy-five-pound shepherd on its back. With great effort, we pulled and poled our way through the swamp, the four-by-eight-foot sheets catching on grasses and bushes.

By the time we got to the upper end of the pond, Karl and Linda had made several trips with their packs and gave us a hand with unloading. We spent a sweaty two hours carrying particle boards and equipment the rest of the way to the cabin site. The sheets dug into our shoulders and banged into branches. The

"Pioneer" helper Ricky and I enjoy lunch on the newly finished floor of
the cabin.

packs sagged with the weight of the rest of the gear, plus jars of
peanut butter, jelly, and Gatorade.

At the site, surprisingly, Ricky proved to be a powerhouse of
energy and skill. He had already climbed forty-four of the Adirondack High Peaks over four thousand feet and knew how to rappel,
chop wood, make fires, and camp. The two of us dragged in a
dozen logs, then began notching and laying them up as sides of
the cabin. It was slow, tedious work as we rolled each log back and
forth until the saddle fitted well over the log below. Karl and
Linda measured the floor opening and cut joists and particle
sheets to fit.

By the end of that weekend the walls were almost two feet
high and the ten-by-ten-foot floor was firmly in place. We celebrated by using it as our table for lunch. But midway through, big

raindrops began falling and thunder rumbled in the distance. We crowded into my old tent (left standing to store equipment in) and waited out the storm. To pass the time, we made up names for this book. In the group effort, amid booms of thunder, most seemed funnier and more inspired than they did later. A few samples: "Condor and Woodswoman—Endangered Species"; "Miles Deeper"; Deer Fly Haven"; "Wilderness Whimsy"; "Is Woods-woman Miss Piggy?"; "Is Seclusion Still Possible?"; and "Lilypad Lament—The Woodswoman's Answer to Society."

When the storm subsided, we crawled out. Karl pointed proudly to his floor. It fitted so perfectly that the water had collected and formed a pool three inches deep.

"Well," I remarked, "even if we never finish this cabin, it can be used as a swimming pool or wading pond."

"Or a hot tub or Jacuzzi." The kids chimed in. Little did I know the words might become a minor prophecy of what would befall Thoreau II.

My second work party was dedicated to dragging more logs into the site and laying up the walls. My good friend Mary came with her brother and boyfriend. Mary worked as a librarian and was an avid reader. Despite her slightly bookish air, she was an expert outdoorswoman with strong shoulders and thighs, thanks to countless hours of jogging and weight lifting. Her brother was equally strong and athletic. I knew they would be a tremendous help in lifting logs to the higher levels.

Mary's boyfriend was a city person, born and bred. He came from Montreal and was fine-boned, yet he pitched in like a lumberjack. I was enchanted by his French accent and droll sense of humor. Again, we spent hours packing in the usual gear, plus a stout door, several mismatched windows, old screens, and some odd lengths of two-by-eights for framing. This time I absolutely prohibited Condor from riding in the canoe, for the windows lay across the gunwales. I didn't need shattered glass inside the craft, cutting us and my dog. As it was, it took all the skill and care we could muster to carry them intact to Thoreau II. My dog, however, was to get his revenge for being left on the shore.

So far everything taken up to the building site was cast-off, old, donated, or scrounged stuff. The only expenses I had were for nails, gas, and oil—perhaps a total of ten or twelve dollars. Even the spikes were free. They were the ones Condor and I had found and packed out of the woods two years before. We used them to secure the corners of the cabin walls together.

While the two men cut and pulled in logs, Mary and I worked together on the walls. We got into a steady rhythm of notching our ends of a log, rolling it over to try its fit, rolling it back up for fine adjustments, then spiking the two saddles onto the log below. I finished by running my chain saw sideways along the crack to remove any knots, knobs, or loose bark where the sphagnum moss

My friend Mary and I hard at work on the walls of Thoreau II.

or fiberglass chinking would eventually go. Mary, meanwhile, hooked a new log and hoisted it over the side and into place for the next round. Building Thoreau II was an easier job than West of the Wind because the logs were only half the size. But while my big cabin had risen a foot for every log laid in place, it took three logs to make a foot at the baby cabin.

By the end of *this* weekend the walls were four feet high. Wearily we packed up and started toting things back to Black Bear Lake. It meant making two trips by canoe. On the first one we carried chain saws, gas cans, and cameras. On our second paddle down Birch Pond there were only a few heavy tools to transport. As Mary and I slipped through the marsh, I glanced back and saw a black muzzle, two gleaming eyes, and a pair of erect ears swimming swiftly behind the canoe. Condor was determined *not* to be left behind. He caught up, whined, shot one paw toward the gunwale, and rolled us into the water. The yellow canoe flopped as effortlessly as a flounder. Mary and I stood sputtering in four feet of chilly, muddy water while Condor continued swimming nonchalantly down the channel. When we stopped laughing, we had the distasteful job of plunging our heads and arms underwater to retrieve axes, pry bar, hammers, and maul. Luckily Mary did not lose her horn-rimmed glasses, but she looked like Medusa with her dripping locks of hair.

I scheduled a third pioneer work party for early September, hoping to get the walls up to six and one-half feet. That would enable me to get the rafters and roof on before the cold weather and heavy rains started in October. This time an older couple came to help. Only Hank was able to work since his wife, Heidi, was recovering from an operation. Because of this, they would sleep inside cozy West of the Wind while Condor and I snuggled out in the lean-to.

Hank was a stout woodsman and a surveyor by profession. He'd roamed the Adirondacks for years and was a storehouse of local history. The time passed quickly as he recounted all the major land sales and property owners in the area since the original Totten and Crossfield, Macomb, and Old Military tracts purchases in the late 1700s. Meanwhile, his large, square hands moved deftly as he used ax, level, saw, tape measure, and maul with equal ease.

As we worked, Heidi called encouragement from a cushion of jackets and blankets under a big spruce. Her pale face was wreathed with smiles when Hank and I reached the five-foot mark on the log walls. She brought over hot coffee and chocolate-chip cookies while we celebrated with a break.

When we resumed work, fate took a hand. Hank and I were lugging an extra heavy log toward the cabin when one or both of us stumbled. I don't know exactly how it happened, but suddenly the big log fell from our shoulders to the ground. On its way it struck my thigh, bounced once, and slid off. Fortunately it missed our feet.

At first the blow felt like any ordinary thump one gets while working in the woods. I sat down for a few minutes and waited for the pain to ease up. Heidi brought ice from her thermos, wrapped it in a wet bandanna, and I slid my pants down so as to soak my leg. After ten minutes I decided it might be better to keep using the leg so the muscles wouldn't tighten up. I was in too much pain to haul any more logs, but I picked up an ax and started climbing into the shell of the cabin.

"You'd best stop and rest," Hank cautioned. "Let's go back to the big cabin."

"I'm OK," I said obstinately, watching the afternoon light begin to fade away. The thought of fall, its early evenings, and the coming cold made me overly anxious to work as long as possible.

But by 5:00 P.M. my leg was straining inside my jeans, swollen almost half again its size, and it felt very taut. I started slowly down the trail, empty-handed, leaving Hank and Heidi to tidy up and carry out the gear. Before many steps I realized I couldn't reach the cabin without a support of some kind. Hank caught up with me and handed me the two axes. By turning them upside down, I used the heads as cane handles and managed to hobble through the woods.

It was almost dark when we reached Black Bear Lake. I crept indoors, swallowed four aspirins, and sank to the cabin floor. Heidi hurried to fix an ice pack while Hank dragged down the sleeping pad from inside the lean-to to lie on. "You'd better not try to climb into your loft tonight or stay in the lean-to," he said worriedly. "You might not be able to stand up in the morning."

He was right. By morning my thigh was enormous, and I could not walk. Heidi and Hank insisted that I get medical help. Reluctantly I agreed. On the one hand, I wanted to get on with the new cabin construction. On the other, I needed Mike's reassurance and expertise. He'd know what was wrong. All night, as I tossed miserably on the cabin floor, I'd thought of his penetrating steel gray eyes, his wide, warm smile, his strong, sure hands. The throbbing of my leg brought back the sense of helplessness I had felt when injured. The fact that I had no family to turn to, no relatives to call for help frightened me. I yearned for a friend, for Mike's friendship.

Heidi and Hank offered to accompany me to Mike's office, but I stubbornly insisted on two cars. I would drive my truck with Condor in it. After a great deal of maneuvering and pain, I squeezed into the driver's seat with my left leg out straight. Heidi packed my leg with pillows, as protection against the bumpy mountain roads. Luckily I had an automatic shift, so I could drive with just the right leg.

En route we stopped for a fast-food milk shake, to buy more aspirins, and to call Mike. Since I dared not move out of the truck, we parked our cars in a little town park overlooking a lake. Hank let Condor out to run. Immediately he headed into the water for a swim. How I envied him. My leg burned and throbbed constantly, and I was faint with anguish. Could I possibly have broken it?

Engrossed with the pills and the milk shake, I didn't notice when Condor came out of the lake, shook himself, and rolled around on a strip of sand. He came back to the truck and hopped in. Then an overpowering stench of rotten fish hit me like a fist!

Tears sprang to my eyes, and I lowered my head to the steering wheel. How much more could go wrong? I wondered as my stomach churned. Heidi hurried over, took a breath, and reeled backward. Then Hank arrived to save the situation. He sped to the nearest grocery store and came back with two cans of tomato juice and a bottle of Ajax detergent. While we two women watched—one giggling, one groaning—he poured the juice over Condor, let it set for a few minutes, and gave the dog two sudsy baths and a rinse in the lake. That rascal still reeked to high heaven, but at least the stench was now tolerable, and I could permit him in the same vehicle with me.

That crisis over, Hank placed a call to Mike's office. After Mike heard about my problem, he told Hank to go right to the emergency room at the hospital. Upon arrival, an hour later, I was eased out of my truck and into a wheelchair, then rolled off for X rays. Mike popped in, glanced at the plates, and made a quick examination.

Nothing was broken. There was, however, a massive hematoma and muscle damage. Mike ordered bed rest for two weeks, plus another two weeks of taking it easy with crutches and cane.

I stared at him, then at Heidi and Hank. Where was I to recuperate? At my cabin? That was clearly impossible. How could I climb the ladder to my sleeping loft, carry buckets of drinking water from the lake, make my way on crutches to the outhouse, chop and carry firewood?

"You can come home with us," said Heidi, reading my

thoughts, "but that means another three hours of driving. And I'm still kind of wobbly from my operation. Hank has to tend to all the housework plus his full-time job."

I shook my head. "No, Heidi, it's too much of a burden for you." I said. "Probably the best thing is for me to go to a local motel."

"Why don't you stay at my camp?" Mike said slowly. "It's empty most of the time now since my divorce. No one will bother you, and the dog will be safe outside. It's all on one floor, so it will be easy for you to get around."

I stared at him in astonishment as Hank and Heidi smiled with relief. What a generous offer from this superbusy physician. And suddenly I sensed a deeper thread of feeling between us. Could it be that Mike's heart had missed a beat, too, somewhere along the way? Or was he simply extra sorry for me? He was such a dedicated physician, and it could be pity. Impulsively I accepted his invitation. It was the only way, I told myself, to get back on my feet again.

Thus I recuperated in a comfortable, all-electric, new Adirondack camp, a place of luxury compared to my cabin. By day I busied myself with writing, catching up on correspondence, reading, and snatching the last of summer's sun. Every other evening Mike stopped by with his black bag to check on my leg. He brought TV dinners, newspapers, dog food, outrageous sweets, and medicine as needed. These had to be the most pleasant house calls any patient ever received!

More than anything, Mike brought himself. Away from the tremendous pressures of his medical world, he seemed to relax at his camp with me. He was laconic, low-key, courtly, almost shy. He told about a strange new world to me, the one he was totally immersed in: medicine. In turn, I shared woodland adventures with him. He even read *Woodswoman*—the first book he'd finished in years, he said. Most of his reading involved keeping up with medical journals. Despite our vast personal differences, age gap, and professional responsibilities, we formed a fragile bond. The sensation of being so well cared for took getting used to, after my years of self-reliance. It had been so long since I'd left a man get close to me or let myself get close to a man. I had come to the conclusion that my independence and career were the safest goals to pursue. Apparently the same had become true for Mike.

When my leg was healed enough so I could manage back at the cabin, I began to make preparations to leave. One rainy September night Mike said tentatively, "Have you ever thought of spending the winter away from your cabin? It must be awfully harsh and lonely there. Would you, by chance, like to come back and spend the winter here?" His voice trailed away. "I'd like to have you," he added.

I waited a moment before answering. It seemed so natural, so logical, so acceptable. Much as I would miss my cabin, I realized I would miss Mike more. So I agreed.

When I returned to West of the Wind, it was early October. The spell of *bad* luck had convinced me to stop work on my beloved Thoreau II. I had only half a haven to show for all the hard work and the pioneer parties. And now another whole season must pass before I could return to finish it. However, the spell of *good* luck with Mike balanced it out. He was offering me a haven for half a year—with love.

One crisp autumn day Hank and Heidi came back to help me cover the little log structure for the winter. We laid the rafters over the five-foot walls and blanketed this makeshift roof with plastic. The ten-by-ten-foot square looked lifeless and useless, staring up at the sky. It was too tall to be a pool or a tub, as I'd joked with Karl about; too short to be a house. There was no doorway or windows. It was simply an empty shell. Only a homeless porcupine might find shelter there overwinter.

I limped back to Black Bear Lake with my friends, and I put

Thoreau II out of my mind. It would not do to dwell on what had happened. I had a busy winter ahead and an exciting man to get to know. I had to believe everything was happening for the best. I packed up the most necessary belongings and trucked them down to Mike's camp. If I needed anything during the winter, I could always drive back and snowshoe in for them. By early November I was cozily settled. I regained the use of my leg with barely a mark or twinge to show for that mighty thump. Life took on a new pattern.

Two nights a week and usually on weekends Mike would come stay at his camp. I'd prepare a simple, wholesome meal with lean meat, salad, boiled rice or potatoes, full-grain breads, and no desserts. Yet often Mike would bustle in with bags brimming with coffee cake, ice cream, munchies, TV dinners, white bread, and Coke. Our eating habits were totally different, but I secretly enjoyed splurging on junk foods once in a while.

After supper I might show him slides of my conservation work and foreign travel. This in itself was a treat for me, being able to plug in my slide projector. Or we might discuss one of my articles or some aspect of medicine or watch TV. We rarely went out to dinner, for he was always on call.

I kept the camp clean, shoveled walks, raked leaves, hauled firewood, cared for Condor, did laundry, and otherwise combined the tasks that a man and woman living together would normally share. Yet I wanted to spare Mike. I knew how busy he was helping people. Besides, having been desperately in need of a doctor, *that* doctor, three times, how could I possibly complain when he was hours late seeing patients or called away on an emergency operation?

Living in an all-electric camp was ridiculously easy compared to my gas, wood, and candles cabin. Even though I kept pushing the wrong buttons on the almond-colored stove, and getting strange rings, cooking here did not require hauling two-hundred-pound propane tanks by boat and connecting them. Doing the wash in the almond-colored laundry set was as simple as setting two dials in the back room rather than driving fifty miles round trip to the public Laundromat. I could read with three-way bulbs in lamps that always worked and make calls on the touch telephones that were everywhere. No need to visit Sally and Sid and my answering machine. A fine vacuum made cleaning the shaggy rugs and hardwood floors child's play compared to my broom-and-shake routine at the cabin.

In short, Mike had a built-in support system at his camp just as he did in his office and operating room. That was the way he lived, having things handed to him or done for him, while he performed the most exquisite of human skills—delicate operations on critically ill human beings. It was a totally new way of life for this self-reliant woodswoman. I began to wonder if the hardy part of me might start rubbing off overwinter.

Meanwhile, Thoreau II lived in my heart and dreams. At night I dreamed of it. During boring meetings I fantasized over its construction. When homesick, I daydreamed about living there the following spring and fall. I pictured the tiny cabin surrounded with fresh green ferns, or framed with autumn leaves, or mantled by snow, smoke wafting from the stovepipe. I resolved to complete my half a haven in 1985. That was the centennial of the Adirondack Forest Preserve, so it seemed a thoroughly appropriate time to finish and christen my retreat.

The state portion of our six-million-acre park had been set aside and declared "forever wild"* in 1885 by a sagacious piece of

---

*"The lands now or hereafter constituting the Forest Preserve shall be forever kept as wild forest lands. They shall not be sold, nor shall they be leased or taken by any person or corporation, public or private"—Chapter 283 of the Laws of 1885; May 15, 1885, now Article XIV of the State Constitution.

legislation. Therefore, in 1985, along with politicians, bureaucrats, scientists, and conservationists, I would celebrate this treasured chunk of real estate and my own forever wild sanctuary within it. It would be an auspicious year to start living like Thoreau.

All in all, it was a winter of contentment.

10

My Nuclear Winter

W *It happened* down at the public landing one afternoon when I took my garbage out to the Dumpster. As I pulled up to the dock, I noticed a dark van with government plates drive away. It's unusual enough to see state cars here—state troopers, conservation officers, or health officials—let alone *federal.* Must be someone doing acid rain research, was my first thought.

While I was opening the Dumpster lid, a neighbor couple walked by. We chatted a few moments, and then I made some reference to the van.

"Oh, them!" the woman said knowingly. "There's four of them, and they've been wandering all over these woods the last few days. Haven't you seen 'em up at your place?"

"No," I replied. "Why are they doing that?"

"Well, it's something to do with rocks." She lowered her voice conspiratorially. "And something to do with the nuclear."

"The nuclear what?" I asked.

"A nuclear waste survey." Her husband chimed in. "At least that's what their clipboards say. They sure didn't want *us* to see them. Kept shoving things on top of the papers. But Martha here, she's real keen-eyed. Used to shoot deer, you know. She cozied up to one of them fellers. Asked to see the little hammer and pick he had in his pack. That's how she got a glimpse of what was on the clipboard."

Martha nodded sagely. "Their packsacks were full of rocks, and they said they were making a geological survey."

Warning bells began clanging in my head. A nuclear waste survey? What could be going on at Black Bear Lake? I knew the time was running out for the two federal high-level nuclear waste repositories in South Carolina and Washington. But the Adirondacks, especially the isolated sections around my cabin, seemed the least likely spot anyone would *ever* consider for dumping of wastes.

I was to find out more at the next Adirondack Park Agency meeting, where we were informed that the U.S. Department of Energy was searching for new nuclear disposal sites. These would replace the other two when they closed on or shortly after January 1, 1986. The department's Office of Civilian Radioactive Waste Management, Crystalline Repository Project Office was combing the entire country for potential places. Two criteria for safe repositories were (1) that no escape of radionucleotides would be possible for at least ten thousand years and (2) that no volcanic activity had taken place in the past one million years.

The Adirondack Park and adjacent areas were at the top of the list because they contain a high percentage of all the crystalline rock formation in the East. This rock, so we were told, is hard, old, stable, and deep granite. The geological formation is known as the Canadian shield, and it underlies vast sections of eastern Canada, cropping out again in the Adirondack Mountains of upstate New York. Other acceptable sites in this nation are in Texas, Utah, Mississippi, Louisiana, Washington, and Nevada.

We commissioners were shown conceptual designs of 980-

The Adirondacks, an outcropping of the Canadian Shield, a mass of ancient granites containing large amounts of crystalline rock, are under consideration as a high-level nuclear waste repository.

foot-plus-deep shafts which would be drilled into the ground and fitted with elevators to transport the highly radioactive containers of wastes (mostly spent nuclear plant fuel and industrial and other peacetime nuclear products) into underground caverns. When I saw these diagrams, I suddenly felt as if a *Star Wars* scenario had descended upon these ancient mountains. The nuclear age was right here in my backyard. Acid rain was bad enough, falling, unasked for, upon our countryside. But a storage of nuclear wastes went beyond all reason in a huge pristine public park like this.

After that APA meeting I crawled into my sleeping loft and lay awake for hours, worrying. I pictured how it would be if the repository were to be located near Black Bear Lake. There would be new, wide, smooth highways built to safeguard the transport of highly hazardous materials. There would be heavy construction—shafts drilled, ramps built, high-tension lines laid to operate the elevators, trenches dug for water lines, huge patches of forest covered with asphalt to make areas for parking and storage. There would be months and months of noise, dust, and visual disturbance in this landscape of lakes and hills. Then, finally, the drums and barrels would arrive, day after day, year after year, carrying tons and tons of radioactive uranium, plutonium, curium, and other transuranic wastes. Many of these radionucleotides would stay hot for thousands, perhaps tens of thousands of years, a constant threat to countless generations in the Adirondacks and elsewhere. I imagined a sinister, hollow rumbling like kettledrums creep through that night. Alone in my loft, I protested: No, no, no!

But what could one person do to stop such a project? What impact could an individual have against a huge, powerful government agency and against the most malevolent of materials ever devised by humankind? Other "environmental crusades"—for endangered species and threatened habitats, against acid rain, water pollution, and pesticide spraying—seemed easy to wage compared to the magnitude of this one.

Nevertheless, I resolved to try to do *something*. Otherwise how could I live with myself in my own home? How could I sleep peacefully at night if I remained a passive onlooker? Other people had to be notified and warned about this new menace to the Adirondacks.

I started talking to friends, writing to colleagues. I asked questions at the next APA meeting of staff and other commissioners. I learned that many people cared as much as I did. The senior staff of the park agency put together a clear, concise statement of concern to the Department of Energy, requesting that the Adirondack State Park and private lands be excluded from consideration as a disposal site.

The statement was based on two main arguments. One was the general *lack* of information about rock erosion and stability, earthquake hazards, groundwater conditions, and crustal deformations in the eastern United States, particularly in the Adirondacks. Should any engineering mistakes lead to radioactive leaks from any caverns, contamination of any one of the five major watersheds in New York state which head up in the Adirondacks might occur. The result might be contamination of drinking and domestic water of millions of people and animals in the state.

The second argument related to the Department of Energy's own guidelines, which exclude *national* parks as sites. The APA's statement demonstrated that the Adirondack *State* Park (Forest Preserve) is just as valuable a resource as—if not more valuable than—most *national* parks. For one thing, any five national parks in the continental United States can fit inside our mammoth six-million-acre sanctuary, making ours the largest park in the lower forty-eight states. For another, we boast 20 percent of all designated wilderness east of the Rockies; 20 percent of the wild, scenic, and recreational rivers in the nation; and almost three thousand lakes and ponds. Moreover, the park is ringed with large population centers and hosts up to ten million tourists a year.

One of our agency attorneys took this document to Albany and presented it at a Department of Energy meeting. He returned with an *oral* agreement that the park would be excluded. However, he cautioned us: "Wait till you see it in print officially in the *final* DOE guidelines. Anything can happen between now and then."

Shortly after this episode there was another "radioactive event" at APA. In our monthly packet of applications for new projects requiring permits, one stood out like a red flag. It was a laboratory which would be using radioactive isotopes as tracers in medical research. The lab wanted permission to store carbon 14 and tritium at the building and to dispose of radioactive liquid wastes down the drain. From the lab sink, these would enter the local sewer system and the sewer plant and eventually flow as effluent into an adjacent river.

I knew that the half-life of C_{14} was 5,700 years and of H_3 was 12.3 years, so these isotopes would not exactly disappear overnight once they had entered the ecosystem. It seemed to me that they might accumulate, disperse, enter living animals and plants in the food chain, and eventually end up in Lake Champlain. But we were told that the amounts to be dumped were negligible and effects would be minuscule.

I asked a lot of questions. What could happen to the summer people who had cottages all along the river corridor? These people swam and fished in river water, drank it, and washed dishes with it. Could C_{14} or H_3 be absorbed by algae, turtles, loons, or otters? Might these isotopes pile up in the mud or accumulate within the water column? What were the danger levels for humans? Who checked the river for radioactivity?

Nobody had all the answers. In fact, it became apparent that my fellow commissioners and I didn't know a microcurie from an X ray from an alpha particle. We were lost in the nuclear age. What I did sense, however, was that we were hearing the same saw we'd heard about "solving" the acid rain problems: "The solution to pollution is dilution." Just as fossil fuel emissions are mingled in the airstream for them to "disappear," so dirty radioactive wastes would be mixed with river water to make them go away.

To my amazement, most members of the committee who handled permits voted to approve this little lab's project for economic reasons! How could the APA commissioners in one breath fully endorse keeping *high-level* rad wastes out of the park yet condone letting *low-level* wastes stay in? Moreover, we had a legal mandate to protect water quality in the Adirondacks, *not* to allow its deterioration. Pouring radioactive isotopes down the drain was hardly obeying our own law!

I said all this to the full agency membership next day, and more. "We're only seeing the tip of the nuclear iceberg," I predicted. "This may be the first such application, but it won't be the last. There are already about a dozen other research facilities, hospitals, and labs scattered through the Adirondacks which were built years ago. They're probably using radioactive isotopes, and we don't realize it. And more will come. Scientific research is a so-called clean industry that can help our local economy. The APA has no jurisdiction over such activities, other than the water protection mandate. We should contact the Department of Health to find out what's really going on."

My arguments worked. The full agency overruled the earlier committee decision and voted to have the little lab's radioactive wastes transported *out* of the park.

Before long, our staff discovered, to everyone's amazement, ten other Adirondack institutions which were using a total of twenty-five different radioactive isotopes in research or medical work. How these were disposed of was not exactly clear. Some were trucked out, some incinerated, some stored, and some dumped locally down drains. We also learned that the local river was checked only once every three years for radioactivity. This disclosure opened a Pandora's box.

Articles on radioactivity were sent out for us to read. State officials were invited to speak to the agency. The two state departments assured us that the amounts in use and disposed of in the park were "small and insignificant." They assured us there was nothing to worry about.

Frankly I was skeptical. Too little was known; too little was monitored. I personally wanted more information. Besides, it seemed to me that the public trust was being violated if we allowed so much as one microcurie loose in this beautiful park where people came to play, relax, and feel healthy. I kept hounding our poor staff to obtain more data. Because of other pressing work, it took some time to gather the information.

Meanwhile, in March the National Wildlife Federation held its annual meeting in Washington, D.C. In my capacity as a director-at-large I decided to submit a resolution calling for the complete exclusion of the Adirondack State Park as a high-level nuclear waste repository. I reasoned that the country's largest and wealthiest conservation group might carry some clout with the administration and such a resolution could add one more bit of ammunition to our campaign to protect the park.

At the convention I found to my chagrin that many of the state delegates wanted either to *add* their natural state areas to our Adirondack resolution or to *strip* names of any specific parks from it. I nicknamed the two factions the Christmas Tree Trimmers, and the Day-After-Christmas Strippers. I spent three hectic days talking, cajoling, defending, and arguing with individual delegates and the Energy Resolutions Committee members. Some folks were sympathetic to my cause; others, downright antagonistic. It was my first brush with the not-in-my-backyard syndrome in relation to nuclear waste disposal.

At the general session on the last day all the new resolutions were read and voted upon by the entire group of state affiliate directors. There was a sudden new flurry of activity between the Trimmers and Strippers when "my resolution" came up. The chair prevailed, explaining we'd been all over this for hours. The resolution passed, with Canyonlands National Park and the Great Lakes watershed tacked onto the Adirondack Park to be excluded.

I felt triumphant and exhausted. The experience had projected me from a regional worry about my homeland to a national concern for any significant natural area that might come under the scrutiny of the Department of Energy.

Sometime later the Department of Energy's final draft guidelines *did* come out and *did* disqualify both national and state parks. I hoped that these guidelines would become permanent and protect the Adirondack Park for all time.

Meanwhile, back at the APA, information had accumulated on the amounts and uses of those twenty-five radioactive isotopes in the park. A great many were applied in genetic and cellular research and in nuclear medicine at local labs and hospitals. We now learned about this new and different application of radiation.

In the United States today close to ten million doses of radioactive pharmaceuticals and X rays are given to patients yearly by doctors, radiologists, and dentists. This *medical* exposure almost equals the amount of *natural* radiation which human beings normally receive annually from the sky, rocks, and other sources. In the Adirondacks, so far as we knew, the biggest source of ionizing radiation *at present* is not wastes from research facilities but from medical exposure. I saw no problem with that. Everyone wants and needs high-tech health remedies to safeguard and prolong life. The problem lay with the *disposal* of these low-level radioactive isotopes after use.

Now came a surprise twist. We found out that every person who is treated with radioactive isotopes or gets a special scan carries this radioactivity out of the hospital and into the everyday world. His or her inner radiation is released gradually via urine, sweat, feces, breath, and saliva into the air and sewer systems. In fact, it was said that just one patient's evacuation in the toilet at home could show up in a town sewer system and be detected within hours. Radioactive wastes accumulate and decay over hours, days, or months in sewage systems. Many of these radioactive elements have half-lives of sixty days or less (e.g., technetium

99, six hours, and iodine 131, eight days). This means they disappear quite quickly. Others linger and seep into the environment via effluent in water bodies or sludge in landfills, possibly contaminating other forms of life.

Clearly there was no way to control *this* type of radioactive release in the park. The state could not run around making people urinate into special pots and then dispose of them in safe sites. But it *could* get a handle on all the other types of disposal and try to arrive at a regulation to prohibit any and all disposal of high-level and low-level radioactive wastes (other than medical wastes) in the Adirondack Park.

Bringing this about has become my burning ambition and goal. After living in my cabin for twenty years, concerned primarily about bears breaking into my kitchen and trees falling on my roof, I have been suddenly catapulted into space age worries. How could this happen to a simple woodswoman?

Then the APA sent me that winter to an extremely technical conference on low-level nuclear waste disposal and cleanup in Washington, D.C., to find out what, if any, applicable techniques might work up here. It was like a baptism by fire. I heard about the latest federal regulations; the status of the compacts among states for disposal sites; innovative storage facilities; the latest technology in massive compaction and incineration of nuclear wastes; the staggering cleanup costs and case histories of sites that leaked and contaminated adjacent areas.

There wasn't much I could report back to the APA on specific ways to dispose of wastes; everything discussed had been in the hundreds of thousands of tons and millions of dollars. Clearly the country at large is in a sorry plight with regard to the problem of nuclear waste disposal. Our Adirondack situation is a wee drop in the big bucket. The conference gave me a different perspective yet strengthened my resolve to eliminate any future dumping in the park.

Ironically, one of the topics brought up was the national priorities list for the most hazardous radiation sites in the country. There, to my horror, was Montclair/West Orange, New Jersey! I had grown up in Montclair, and my parents had moved to West Orange after I'd left for college. With eerie fascination I read about a radium processing facility that had been in operation in West Orange in the 1920s and how later home builders had used soils from this abandoned site for fill during construction in the 1930s. In 1979 the New Jersey Department of Environmental Protection began investigating such former radium facilities. Overflights by EPA planes disclosed three residential communities with high levels of gamma radiation from rad waste disposal. One of these was Montclair! Had I been unlucky, it might have been right under my house.

In 1983 the Center for Disease Control issued a public health advisory for these areas, to alert officials and people to the risk of breathing indoor radon gas, high gamma exposure, and potential radium ingestion. In 1984 ventilation systems were installed in twenty-two houses to blow fresh air into their basements. By 1985 the state was starting an eight-million-dollar cleanup project which involved excavating, moving, and disposing of up to fifteen thousand cubic yards of contaminated soil from twelve yards.

When I heard of this, the lesson from my hometown was clear: Don't ever *start* nuclear waste disposal in the Adirondacks. That way we can avoid any such colossal cleanup expenditure and public hazard in the future.

As winter slowly yielded to spring, the last of the events that made up my "nuclear winter" occurred. Indeed, it *was* nuclear winter. My editor at Norton sent me a book entitled *The Cold and the Dark*, by Paul R. Ehrlich and Carl Sagan, Donald Kennedy and Walter Orr Roberts. It contained the most up-to-date reports and scientific conjectures of American and Soviet scientists about the catastrophic consequences of nuclear war.

I read how smoke and dust released by nuclear blasts and their afterfires would cast a pall that would block most sunlight. Atmosphere, climate, and weather patterns over most of the earth would be severely affected. Temperatures would plummet, plants freeze, animals and humans starve. There would be no summer for a long, long time. In addition to the cold and dark, all life would be exposed to high-radiation ultraviolet light (owing to the depletion of the ozone layer) and toxic gases set free from the burning of many synthetic materials. When the sun eventually returned, many terrestrial animals might go blind in the new, unfiltered glare. In short, the elegant, balanced ecosystems of earth would be devastated.

Needless to say, the Adirondacks would become a Siberia. (It's hard enough to grow crops and keep warm here now what with our climate.) Could Thoreau have possibly realized the portent of his words when he wrote in *Walden:* "nor need we trouble ourselves to speculate how the human race may be at last destroyed. It would be easy to cut their threads any time with a little sharper blast from the north. . . . [A] little colder Friday, or greater snow, would put a period to man's existence on the globe"? He knew nothing of nuclear winter, yet he knew the fragile lifeline to which humanity clings.

The effect of my exposure to nuclear winter was to drive home once and for all the realization I could not escape even in my wilderness cabin. I would be as vulnerable as someone living in Manhattan or Moscow. Yet this more realistic and sober attitude did not deter me from wanting to finish my retreat. It merely changed the focus of my dream. I perceived how people *need* pieces and places of privacy more than ever before. They need to blot out the specters hanging over humanity for bits of time. They need Thoreau IIs wherever, whenever, and however they can find or fashion them.

11

Thoreau II

On a windy, raw, rainy June day—more reminiscent of October than the start of summer—I walked up to Thoreau II alone. I portaged the yellow canoe to its tiny harbor on Birch Pond, then cleared the trail of winter debris. Finally I lugged in the first load composed of my old blue tent with its poles, a huge sheet of plastic as groundcloth, and stakes. In this I'd store tools, boots, ax, nails, gas, and other work items necessary for completing the cabin retreat.

As I paddled quietly up the pond with Condor at the alert in the center of the canoe, my emotions were mixed. I felt both exuberant to be headed back after eight months and rueful over the situation. The combination of APA restrictions, acid rain damages, and nuclear waste apprehensions would make my building somewhat more symbolic than functional. But these thoughts were short-lived. Suddenly a nesting mallard mother jumped out of the grass. She treated us to a superb act of subterfuge to lure the craft away from her eggs. Noisily flapping her wings, she wobbled away as if injured just ahead of the canoe. A group of rusty blackbirds raised a ruckus as we slid past their nest sites. Swallows were soaring over the still, ebony water. They would fly upward with their breasts puffed out and wings back like a diver executing a full swan dive, then swoop down to the surface and make several erratic turns. Water boatmen were zigzagging merrily over the pond until they were picked off neatly by the birds at the climax of their swan dives.

The yellow blossoms of cow lilies were already floating among the oval pads. As we swished through them, I noticed that almost half had been snipped off, leaving jagged stalks. Evidently beavers came here each evening for dessert. I imagined them browsing leisurely through the pads, placidly popping the golden balls into their mouths like caramel popcorn.

Curious about the taste, I snapped a blossom off and nibbled it bit by bit. The four petals were astringent, and the bulbous part was sharply bitter. I decided a cow lily tasted rather like a wild dill pickle.

After the canoe ride the dog and I walked on to the cabin site at Lilypad Lake. The pond lay wind-ruffled, pearl gray, and peaceful. Near shore a loon floated! Its head was tucked sideways, and it rode the ripples sleepily. It was the perfect welcome, the ideal omen. I'd never seen a loon on Lilypad before. Surely it meant good luck.

When the tent was up, I retraced my steps for a second load. This time I carried two four-by-eight-foot sheets of R Max insulation covered with aluminum foil, plus two sawhorses. Light as two feathers, I balanced the sheets atop my head as far as the canoe, then laid them across the gunwales. Next the sawhorses were crammed in the stern, where I perched gingerly on them. The dog had to run along the shore this time because there was no room in the small craft.

As I finished this portion of my trip, it began to rain. I got out, set one sheet on my head as an umbrella, and balanced a sawhorse on my left shoulder. Awkwardly I bumbled through the woods, trying not to crash into trees and rip the foil on branches. The first trip went well, but on the second I slipped sideways on a wet rock. The sawhorse thumped me on the head, and the insulation slid down my shin, skinning it. Then it broke in three pieces. Gone was my maxiumbrella.

I continued limping to Lilypad with my load, getting wetter by the moment. Disgruntled, I dumped everything next to the tent and headed home. The downpour increased. Condor and I arrived home soaked to our skins and with my pockets stuffed full of torn foil picked off the trail. But even though I was cold and hungry and had a lump on my head, the trip had been a winner as far as I was concerned. The loon at Lilypad had made it so.

That weekend, my librarian friend Mary came to help me "unwrap" Thoreau II. We would take off the makeshift roof of logs and plastic which had protected the shell all winter. We also planned to sort the cut logs into piles for rafters and for the wall. Then we'd know how many more trees were needed to complete the construction.

It was another rainy day. Mary stashed our lunch of hard-boiled eggs, bread, lettuce, salt, and soft drinks in the tent. I unpacked a can of chain saw oil, gas, axes, and a pry bar from our pack baskets. It was almost the identical load of tools that we'd fished out of the marsh the previous fall when Condor tipped over the canoe.

Together we uncovered the cabin-to-be, sorted the logs, and put oil and gas in the chain saw. When it came time to eat, it was still drizzling, so we crawled inside the tent. The eggs were nowhere to be found. Also, a dark puddle of oil lay soaking into the tent floor. The culprit appeared to be a wild weasel. It could easily have sneaked into the tent, tipped over the can, and filched our lunch. We munched halfheartedly on bread and lettuce, then decided to start back early and enjoy a big dinner.

By this time mist was settling over the lake and silvering the spruces. The shoreline looked like a Japanese painting. "Before we go, Mary," I said, "do you mind if I cut a couple of small dead trees away from the edge of the lake? I'd like to improve the view."

"Sure," she answered, though she was shivering slightly. "Want me to take any pictures?"

"Of course," I replied, grateful for her offer. "I never seem to get any shots of myself using a chain saw or ax since I'm usually behind a camera."

Quickly I buzzed down two spruces. Both fell in the water. Their dead branches stuck up bizarrely in the air. "I'll just cut them into sections," I called, "so things don't look so messy. I can drag them out later."

I waded into the shallows in my rubber boots and zipped off some branches. These I placed ahead of me, one atop the other, to make a sort of island on which I could stand in the deeper water. Mary stood onshore and snapped pictures. I stepped out farther and kept sawing, maintaining good balance as I leaned over the horizontal trunk.

"Look this way," yelled Mary, gesturing with the camera.

I turned, smiled, and fell headfirst into two feet of water, with the chain saw running full tilt! It stopped instantly. I picked myself out of the lake, sputtering. Strings of algae hung from the saw blade. Water ran in rivulets from my elbows and sloshed over my boot tops. Mud smeared my face. On top of that, it began raining in earnest.

The two of us trudged back to the cabin, followed by the grumbling dog. "You and I seem doomed to get wet up here," Mary remarked later, after some dry clothes, a hot fire, two Jack Daniel's, and a steak feast had put us in fine spirits.

After supper I worked on my beloved old Homelite saw, removing the spark plug, pulling the rope to eject any water in the carburetor, pouring out the gas and oil, and setting it by the stove to dry. Yet, despite these ministrations, the next morning the damn thing wouldn't start. Mary dropped the saw at a mechanic's shop on her way home. The bill was forty-two dollars! The "unwrapping" of Thoreau II had been a bit expensive.

Now I began to organize pioneer work parties every other weekend to speed up cabin construction. The first group to arrive was an American family whom I'd known in Central America during one of my assignments there. Jack and Margy still lived abroad but were taking a three-week vacation in the States. As part of their trip they came to West of the Wind to camp and help with the new cabin.

They now were a lively family of six including two new babies. That meant that Margy was busy with infants while Jack and the two older children worked with me. Our first chore was to carry seventeen-foot-long one-inch-thick boards up to the cabin for use on the roof. Everyone took as many as he or she could reasonably carry on his or her shoulders. The towheaded, blue-eyed girl had one; the blond, tanned boy, two; I, three; Jack, four. We started walking single file through the woods like so many giant, flapping birds. At Birch Pond I slid each board into the canoe, leaving space for Jack to paddle in the stern and his son Jackie to straddle them in the bow. I warned them how tippy the craft was. Jack stepped in and sat down. Young Jackie followed. Only he stepped off center, and the canoe capsized immediately, flipping father and son onto their backs in the muddy bay. While they were wringing out their shirts, thunder began rumbling.

"Let's go back," I suggested, "and get you dried off."

"No way!" said Jack gallantly, although he was still amazed by the swiftness of his somersault. "I'm wet now, and so is Jackie, so we might as well keep going. Besides, we haven't been in a canoe for years. OK, Jackie?"

His son nodded eagerly. They retrieved the floating boards, emptied out the canoe, and stored them back inside. Carefully the two got in and shoved off while lightning flashed and the heavens opened. It was impossible to stop them. The little girl and I slopped through the gloomy, dripping woods to meet them at the other end. So, with much squishing and sloshing, the roof boards got delivered.

The next day we notched and fitted a few logs for the cabin walls so the kids could see how real pioneers had built their houses. Thoreau II came up to the top of my head. Even diminutive Margy walked and the two blond babies toddled up to see *la casita en el bosque.* All in all, it was an adventurous visit with this warmhearted, good-natured family.

They were due to fly back to Central America the next day, and we carried the baggage down to their station wagon in the morning. Jack fumbled in his pockets for the car keys, then asked Margy if she had them. No. They began looking in the luggage. The kids pitched in. Soon sleeping bags, ponchos, dirty clothes, peanut butter sandwiches, baby toys, and duffel bags were scattered about the parking lot. No keys.

"Don't you have a spare," I asked Jack, "hidden in the car or in your briefcase?"

"No," he said dolefully. "I just bought the wagon for our vacation and didn't have time to make dups."

"Would the dealer have one?"

"No. We didn't buy it from a dealer. It belonged to an old lady on a farm."

Dollar signs started flashing through my head as I estimated the cost of bringing in a tow truck or a mechanic to open the car and make an impression. Jack and his family might be here all day. Conceivably they might miss their plane to Central America.

"The keys have got to be at the cabin," I prophesied.

"Bet they're in the water where Dad fell out of the canoe," Jackie said.

"That's right," Jack replied. "I had on my old jeans, and the three keys were hung on a diaper pin."

"A diaper pin!" I exclaimed, astonished. "Was it pinned to your pants?"

"No," was his crestfallen reply.

"Let's go," I ordered crisply. "We'll find 'em. Margy, maybe you should stay here with the babies and pack up your gear again."

Back at West of the Wind Jackie and I took face masks and a rake and dashed through the woods to Birch Pond. Making extra sure not to stir the mud up, we peered into the water over the sides of the canoe. The bottom was black. No keys. We raked it back and forth, just to make certain.

Meanwhile, Jack and his daughter were searching the cabin, lean-to, paths, and fireplace. After two hours of hunting he found his keys lodged in a crack of the lean-to, where he'd flung his wet jeans after the dunking.

The family was on the road by early afternoon. Everyone was relieved. I retired to my cabin to collapse after the confusion. So much for diaper pins!

The second pioneer work party was to include my friend Cynthia, an attorney from Washington, D.C., and her boyfriend, John. Louise and Dale, a middle-aged local couple, were postal employees. The five of us didn't have a lot in common professionally, yet everyone loved the woods. That's what really counted. Besides, the weather was perfect. We could swim and sail after work, and I'd arranged a big barbecue and campfire Saturday night. My friends wanted to tent out and I'd sleep in the lean-to.

The two women were unskilled in ax, or saw work, so I figured they'd be most useful burning brush and holding logs while I notched and fitted them. The local man, Dale, was strong and woods-wise, but he needed a similar buddy to work with. The men would form a "Clydesdale team" to cut and haul in more logs. I had never met Cynthia's boyfriend. The burning question was what would John be like. Weak; short; fat; timid?

He was none of those things. At six feet five inches, he was a bull of a man with a John Muir beard, who clumped cheerfully into the woods with us and distinguished himself by towing fifteen new logs single-handedly behind a canoe. These had been cut by the two men from a swamp nearby since I'd already taken all the trees I wanted from within an eighth of a mile of Thoreau II.

I wanted to protect my forest and not let it look thinned out or messy from our logging operation. Yet it was getting increasingly hard to find nearby straight, true timber which would make neat, trim walls. So many spruces seemed to have crooks, sways, lumps, and marks or be weakened by insects or acid rain. To help find new trees, I had portaged my other canoe, a red and white Grumman aluminum lightweight up to Lilypad Lake. It was a lot of extra work, but the payoff would be a beautiful landscape around the retreat.

That weekend the walls rose to six feet.

My third and last work party was again with my farm friends Karl, Ricky and Linda. This time Karl brought his ripping chain to use on his saw. He was able to cut logs into flat planks for a camp table and cunning little stools, plus scaffolding, with this. We desperately needed a platform about four feet off the floor to work from because the walls were so high. Since I'm fairly short, it was difficult and dangerous to saw, notch, and spike in the logs once they rose above shoulder height. We also needed a ladder to help with installing the windows and the loft. Ricky and

---

With the aid of a level, Cynthia and I can see how straight the logs are.

Linda began to build a rustic ladder from thin balsam trunks.

It was while Karl and I both were running our chain saws that two A-10 fighter jets roared over the wilderness area and directly above the cabin. The noise was so deafening that we heard it above the saws and protective earmuffs. I shut off my Homelite, flung it down, and shook my fist at the departing planes.

"Bastards," I shrieked, "you're supposed to stay away from the wilderness and this area. Don't you *ever* stop harassing us?"

Karl, meanwhile, had switched off his power saw, looked up, and was cheering the jets. "Attaboys!" he yelled. "What beautiful planes! What technology!" He turned to me, beaming. "I get a real rush watching them."

"But they're not supposed to be practicing war games here, so low and so loud," I protested. "They almost hit a seaplane this summer."

Karl's eyes took on a steely look. "Anne," he said sternly, "when our boys are over Moscow, they have to know what to do." Conversation was strained the rest of that morning as we held our tongues and our opinions to ourselves. Ricky and Linda tactfully dragged their ladder off a little ways and kept quiet.

By lunchtime the episode of the "dueling chain saws" had been dismissed, and we had a fine picnic. A bunch of cedar waxwings perched above us in the spruce tops. They peered down with their black masks and lisped cheerily above the commotion.

Thanks to Karl and his intrepid children, two productive things happened. Because of our disagreement over the jets, I made a concerted effort to stop the training flights over Black Bear and Lilypad lakes. I contacted the commander of the closest Air National Guard base and advised him of our problem with low-flying jets. The property owners' association offered him a boat tour of the area so he could visualize the approaches and routes used by his pilots. This very courteous and helpful officer managed to get a two- to three-square-mile area around our lakes "hatched off" on the aerial maps. This meant that pilots could practice over most of the Adirondacks but were prohibited from flying directly through the airspace above our lands.

The second rewarding event was that the walls of Thoreau II had risen to seven feet and were done. I had left the bark on the round spruce logs. Thoreau had done so, too; only he peeled the interior sides and squared his logs.

The only person *not* to put in an appearance at a pioneer work party was Mike. Although he came to visit me at West of the Wind and good-naturedly tramped up to see the construction, wearing hospital greens and big boots, he showed no interest in helping with the tiny retreat. At first I was disappointed, dismayed. It would have been wonderful to share my new ambition to live like Thoreau with Mike. But on reflection, I realized two things. To work with a chain saw and ax could be hazardous for a surgeon. One slipup, one injury to his hands, might end Mike's career forever. In addition, I came to see that he felt even more isolated from *his* real world up at Lilypad than he did at his comfortable camp or my Spartan cabin. The most natural setting for Mike was an operating room or a hospital ward where he could practice medicine, not in the wilderness, building log retreats.

As a consequence, we didn't see much of each other that summer, yet I continued to miss him and love him.

12

Two Guides

It was time to put on the roof now. One year and three months after I'd started the cabin, it would at last take the shape of a shelter and cease to be a shell. However, I was unsure what type of roof I should build: a slanted trapper style or a peaked chalet style. Each had its advantages and disadvantages.

I turned for advice to Rod, an experienced woodsman and registered guide. We'd known each other for twenty-five years, ever since I'd come to the Adirondacks. Rod had been caretaker at the inn where I first worked as a college student. Over several summers he had watched me gallop on horseback past his cozy clapboard house. My job initially was to care for five horses and teach riding to the hotel guests, so every day I'd ride my mare bareback and lead the other four mounts back and forth to pasture and the hotel stables. Rod always waved a cheery greeting.

Traumatic events had occurred to change our lives since then. I'd been divorced; Rod had lost his wife. He was nearly eighty now, yet as fit, strong, and sharp as a well-honed ax. Rod had built dozens of lean-tos for the state and was a craftsman with a chain saw. He knew all about roofs, I figured. So I stopped to call on him. It seemed to me that a shed type of roof would go up fast, could be built easily by two people, but would afford less room inside the cabin. A gabled roof was more complicated and time-consuming to build yet would offer more interior space.

Rod listened attentively as I talked, nodding and chomping on an evil-smelling cigar. When I was done, he said, "Well, sweet-heart, you better stick with a slanted shed roof. It's simple. You just lay six or seven long rafters across your purlins and then put your roofing boards across. You can have it up in a day."

"Wait a minute, Rod," I said. "What are purlins?"

"Purlins? Why, purlins are purlins," he replied, surprised at my ignorance. "They hold the roof up."

"Oh, I see. Well, sort of." He did make it seem simple. "But, Rod," I groaned, "I've used up all my logs, and I don't want to cut any more trees around the site. How many purlins do I need? How long should they be? How big around?"

The old woodsman paused to relight his stogie. "Don't worry yourself, Annie," he said. "Tell you what. I'll come up there with you and put those purlins on. That's easier than trying to explain it to you."

"Oh, Rod," I exclaimed, with great relief, "that would be wonderful. How much would you charge?"

He shrugged. "Nothin' at all. I'd do it for the fun of it. Be-sides, you're a poor thing. You don't know a purlin from a peavey. I feel sorry for you, getting hurt like that last fall. You need some help or that damn camp'll fall down on your head."

I began to retort, then thought better of it. Acting properly subdued, I agreed to meet Rod at the dock on Black Bear Lake the next morning. He was there promptly at ten o'clock, freshly shaved, and carrying a giant stained pack basket. He lifted a gleaming, razor-sharp, two-bitted ax out of his pickup and stepped confidently toward my motorboat.

"You tell that goddamn dog to lie down and keep quiet," he ordered. "I don't swim. And don't go too fast, Annie. The wind tickles my ears, and there's lots of rocks in this lake."

For a man who'd been born around water and spent his entire life guiding, fishing, and paddling on the lakes, not being able to swim seemed a dangerous handicap. Yet I knew of other Adirondack old-timers who could not swim. Apparently former generations utilized water strictly for ease of transportation when necessary and not for the fun of recreation. Most older men I knew were scared of water. If they would sink upon falling in, this was understandable. I had to hand it to Rod for courage. His inability to swim didn't stop him from traveling by water.

At my cabin we had some coffee and then set out through the woods for the yellow canoe. I wondered how Rod would react to that. Bravely he swung his pack basket and ax aboard but balked when Condor begged to get in. I assured Rod that the dog was canoe-trained and had never tipped me over while inside the craft.

Gingerly he stepped into the tippy canoe, and the shepherd followed. Slowly we paddled up Birch Pond, hugging the shoreline where the water was only waist-deep. Every time that Condor even twitched an ear, Rod would holler out, "Now, set down, you goddamn mutt, or I'll knock your head off with my ax!"

At the cabin he was surprised to see how much work had been done. He did remark on the slight inward tilt of the walls and some of my oversize notches, but "You've done a good job, Annie," was his overall opinion. (This was fine praise from a master builder.) "Now let's get those purlins up," he said energetically.

This was the best time for me while building Thoreau II. Rod

Rodney and Chekika.

and I started working together regularly and made a smooth, though tattered, team. Rod would wear his faded green shirt and pants, with his long johns peeking out even on the hottest days, scuffed boots, and a green felt hat with his old brass guide's button glinting in the sun. (The current buttons were made of cheap, brightly painted tin.) I was usually dressed in my ragged, pitch-smeared jeans, sweat-stained T-shirt, baseball cap, and steel-toed shoes.

I always packed a lunch and tried to surprise Rod with something he especially liked, a cold beer (wrapped in newspaper to keep the chill on) or freshly baked zucchini bread. Munching happily, Rod would praise my "bikini bread" and tell me stories of early encounters with bears, lumberjacks, and storms.

After lunch Rod would light one of his stinking cigars. I'd move a little farther away and lie back briefly to get some sun.

It seemed no time at all before Rod had fallen, limbed, and laid three stout, straight timbers across the cabin walls. These were the famous purlins. The forward two were set high up on posts to give a slant to the roof. Next, I dragged the cut rafters to the building and raised them to Rod on the scaffolding. Together we hefted them into place atop the purlins. Rod notched and leveled them. I spiked them down. Then the roof boards slid smoothly in place and were nailed on. Lastly, I lifted up twelve old, rusty, tarry sheets of roofing steel to cover the twelve-by-sixteen-foot roof.

I had scrounged these sheets from a local dump. Even though they were full of old nail holes, I could tar them shut and use roofing nails with washers to make the whole thing watertight. The cabin looked a little like a lean brown mushroom with an enormous silvery cap.

Rod and I stepped back to admire our work. "It's time to nail a small spruce tree to the center rafter," he declared.

"What for?" I asked.

"For luck. To top off the building."

"But why?" I persisted.

"I dunno for sure," Rod said. "My dad did it. His dad, too, whenever they finished a camp. It's got something to do with being glad no one got hurt on the job and with being grateful for the wood."

"Sounds like a good custom to me, Rod," I said, and complied at once, climbing to the rooftop to nail fast the lucky symbol. Then I made a silent prayer in three parts. One part was to thank the trees I had taken to fashion my retreat. Second was to offer gratitude to Rod, who had helped so much. And the third was to wish that all my days at Thoreau II would be safe, serene, and inspiring.

The crucial moment was behind us, and I felt a tremendous satisfaction at having a roof over my head. The last major piece of

The three purlins, ready for installation at Thoreau II.

construction was to cut out the doorway and windows and frame them in. Doors and windows would give my cabin eyes and a soul. Once there was a way for people and animals to see in and out and walk in and out, life would begin within these four walls.

Rod measured the old door I'd lugged up, then marked the size on the wall with a straight board and a nail upon the logs. Next, he took his chain saw and cut down the two marks. As he reached the bottom log, the short, round sections cascaded onto

Using the chainsaw, and almost finished. The ladder shows where I'll be closing in the sides of the cabin with plywood.

the ground and daylight streamed across the floor. The ends of the cut logs gleamed like golden disks in rows. We pounded in a two-by-ten-inch board as a casing over these ends, cut down the old door to fit, and hung the brass hinges. I stepped across the threshold and entered my home.

In many ways, Rod reminded me of Rob, my old woods pal from Hawk Hill who had taught me to guide. Both men were expert woodsmen, registered guides, and widowed. They were about the same age. Both were short and wiry. But whereas Rob had bright blue eyes, no hair at all, but all his teeth, Rod had dark brown eyes, a thick thatch of hair, and perhaps three teeth. Both men had learned to be self-sufficient about cooking and shopping but drew the line when it came to cleaning and laundry. They hired these chores out.

Memories of Rob always saddened me, for he had died about ten years ago. I was away from the Adirondacks off and on much of that winter. Then I heard that Rob had taken a tumble at the Hawk Hill annual Christmas party. He'd fallen on cement and cracked the tip of his spine. Not realizing the damage done, he'd shuffled home with help from a neighbor. The next day he could hardly move and canceled his daily hike. For two or three weeks he suffered at home, sitting beside the wood stove in his kitchen by day and sleeping in an overstuffed chair near the TV at night. He existed in that confined space and in that bent position, though what he really needed was flat bed rest to mend his break. But he couldn't manage the stairs to his bedroom. Friends brought him groceries, carried in wood, shoveled his walk, and started his car's motor on the sub-zero nights. Since Rob refused to

---

OVERLEAF: Rodney flashing a big smile as he finishes putting in the front—and only—door of the new cabin.

go to the hospital, a county health nurse began checking on him.

The bitter-cold winter days stretched on. Snowmobiles raced up and down the Hawk Hill road. Cross-country skiers occasionally flashed past, but Rob couldn't go outdoors. His daily walk with a pack basket full of mink traps over trails he had trodden for half a century was abandoned. Snow lay deep over his pre-Christmas trapline. Some neighbors discussed setting up a rotating schedule where each neighbor would spend two or three hours a day with Rob. But there weren't enough people to cover the twenty-four-hour period.

His legs began to shrivel from lack of exercise. His appetite decreased. His blue eyes were dull with pain. When his former gusto for an evening boiler maker (a jigger of whiskey in a tall glass of beer) vanished, I knew Rob was deteriorating.

Finally, in March, Rob's son came to take him to a hospital. The son drained the water, turned off the heat, banked the stove, and locked the house. It was the first time in perhaps twenty-five years that the house had stood cold and dark. Rob's traps glinted with frost from their pegs in the back room. His pack basket straps were chewed down gradually by a porcupine until the basket fell from the wall. The red and black wool jacket he always wore in the woods harbored a deer mouse nest in one pocket. The canoe we'd taken up rivers and across lakes fishing was a swollen white lump under the drifts out back.

Gradually the days lengthened and spring tentatively touched the landscape. I came back to Black Bear Lake from my wanderings. Rob was still in the hospital, so one day in May I headed down to see him. I hadn't seen him in weeks. Surely, I thought, his break was healed by now and he was taking physical therapy and walking again. I hoped he could build up his strength enough to try a few short trail walks with me come summer. I knew that healing took time at his age, but being home in his beloved mountains would speed his recovery.

As I rounded a lake on the way, I spied a glorious bush of wild azaleas in full bloom. The delicate blossoms glowed salmon-pink in the strong sun. I pulled off the road and picked several branches of these delicate Adirondack spring flowers. Rob would love them. I stuck them in a pail of water in the back of the truck and drove on.

At the hospital I was dismayed to be directed to a large ward full of old men. The smell of age, stale urine, and creeping death was in the air. I walked briskly forward, my arms full of azaleas, looking for Rob. At first no one seemed to be in the bed the nurse had pointed out. But then I stepped closer and could see a tiny, gaunt body under the tangle of sheets and blankets. I gave an involuntary gasp.

"Rob?" I said softly.

Nothing moved. No one spoke. I reached down and turned on the bedside lamp. The white and blue skeleton that lay on its side in the dim room could *not* be my strong, robust guide friend. The tissuey skin laced with veins could *not* be Rob's. But it *was* Rob —at eighty-two pounds!

"He's not eaten anything for two weeks," the nurse said. "He flatly refuses. We're keeping him going with IVs. But maybe," she said with no real assurance, "he'll eat for you."

"Is he awake?" I asked. "Will he know me?"

"Oh, yes. He's completely aware of what's happening." The nurse let down the side bar of the hospital bed.

I eased onto the mattress, still holding the boughs of blossoms. "Rob?" I whispered.

One fragile eyelid flickered open.

"Rob, look! I brought you some wild azaleas."

He was lying in the fetal position, hands between his legs, and though he barely moved, I knew Rob was alert to my presence. I held the flowers before his face. Did I imagine the ghost of a smile?

"Come on, Rob," I said firmly, "you've got to get out of here.

It's time to go home. We'll go on our hikes again, just as soon as you get your strength back."

The flicker of smile was gone. A dreadful look of resignation passed over his face. Helpless, I sat there. "How about a milk shake?" I suggested, grasping for anything. "Will you drink a milk shake, Rob?"

I gestured to the nurse, who rustled out and came back shortly with a creamy vanilla shake. Slipping her arms under Rob, she slid him effortlessly upward and propped his head on two pillows. Holding the glass and a hospital straw, I began talking to Rob as to a lost, hurt puppy rather than a fearless woodsman. "Come on now. Take a sip. That's it. It'll taste good. Come, Rob. You'll make me so happy."

I pushed the straw between his parched lips. The nurse and I watched as very slowly a strawful of white liquid lifted, bobbled, lowered, and finally rose to his mouth. He took two convulsive swallows. His Adam's apple jerked convulsively. His blue eyes opened, and he gazed at me as if to say he'd done what I asked.

"Drink some more, Rob," I urged. "You've got to build yourself up so we can get into the woods this summer."

He let the straw slip slowly from his lips. "No more," he mumbled, shaking his head feebly.

I realized then that Rob had willed himself to die. Somewhere between Christmas and when he'd entered the hospital, the will to walk again had disappeared. Although his fracture was minor, perhaps Rob envisioned himself unable ever to hike again, imprisoned in his house in a wheelchair, with a walker, on a cane. Maybe he instinctively feared he would never smell the fragrant balsam flats, hear rushing trout streams, feel cool sphagnum moss, or see clear blue lakes reflecting summer clouds.

He'd been independent all his life and so proud of being a guide. His official button was always pinned somewhere to his clothing. This was the one and only way to direct the course of his life as *he* wished it. By simply refusing to eat and drink, he had confounded the doctors, frustrated the nurses, saddened his son, and bewildered his friends. Except for me. I think I would have done the same. He was doing what he wanted—going out with dignity.

Memories of our many trips flooded my mind: There was the stream we'd started down fishing, only to haul out over twenty-two beaver dams and not catch anything; a beautiful four-mile trail that wound us through emerald beaver meadows; the gigantic pine he'd taken me to see and I'd hugged. Once on a local train trip of ten miles, when I was barefoot and he carried his pack basket, a bejeweled lady coming from a Lake Placid resort had mistaken us for hillbillies. In the winter I carried mink traps with him through snowy woods and helped him make the sets. There was a camping trip when I forgot the silverware and we ate spaghetti with spruce twigs. These memories, and so many more.

Rob was sleeping now. I wondered if Adirondack trails wove through his dreams. Did he perhaps wish he were a wounded deer and could sink down under a wild azalea and die? Just do away with all the needles, nurses, and technology that kept him alive artificially?

Silently bereft even as Rob still lived, I slipped out of the hospital. He died not long after my visit. I heard that the azaleas stayed by his bedside until every blossom had dropped. I heard that he spent time every day staring at them.

I never went back to see him. Nor did I go to Rob's funeral. I couldn't handle that either. Instead, I hung his picture in a special place at the cabin. And I pinned to my hat the guide's button given me by his son. Rob was like my grandfather (the one I never

My long-time friend Rob getting ready for some trout fishing. This was before acid rain devastated our lakes.

had) and like my mentor. The Adirondacks would not have become as precious to me without his tutelage. To this day, I treasure my guide's license because Rob taught me this skill and vouched for me on the application. And whenever the wild azaleas bloom, he's strong in my thoughts.

Now Rod had come into my life to help and teach me. He gave me construction knowledge and a snug sanctuary. Despite his rank cigar, his fear of water, and ever-present long johns, he was as much a woodsman as Rob had been. It was as though one neighbor and friend had been reincarnated into the other.

13

Chekika

Condor met the love of his life in Miami. Until then he'd been celibate—not by choice, I hasten to add. But female German shepherds, much less those in heat, seldom came to Black Bear Lake. So Condor's love life had languished in the north woods.

I was going on assignment in the Everglades, and while involved in last-minute preparations, I checked Condor into an air-conditioned kennel. He wasn't used to Florida's heat or traffic, and this seemed kindest. When I came to pick him up, the kennel manager greeted me with "Want to breed your beautiful dog? A lady just called here, looking for a sire. She's got an AKC-registered shepherd that is receptive *now*. She's really eager to have puppies."

For years I'd considered breeding Condor, just to have a puppy with his marvelous genes. Where else would I ever find another dog with his conformation, stamina, patience, and good humor? A puppy would be a safeguard against that future day when Condor would lie next to Pitzi. I hoped never to go through such grief alone without a canine companion in reserve.

I jotted down the woman's number and paid Condor's board. But before taking off, I confided to the kennel manager that I wasn't sure my dog would mate with a strange bitch. "Don't they have to get to know each other?" I asked naïvely. "How will he know what to do? He's seven years old, and has never been . . . Well, you understand what I mean," I added lamely. "Also, Condor has only one testicle. Maybe he can't make puppies."

The kennel owner laughed and slapped me across the shoulder. "Don't worry about a thing, 'Mother,' " he said heartily.

My criteria for Condor's prospective mate were stringent. She had to be beautiful, act nobly, have a gentle disposition, upright ears, and kind eyes. She had to be healthy and free of dysplasia. Firm in my resolve, I left Condor outside the front door as I went to meet the owner and her dog. A rangy, honey-colored female with liquid brown eyes and huge, alert ears sidled up to sniff me. She seemed entranced by the odors on my shirt and shorts. The woman showed me her papers. I saw that the dog's name was Honey.

"This is the only time she'll have puppies," the owner explained. "I'll have her spayed after this litter."

As I hesitated, checking over the papers and examining the possible mother of my puppy, Condor nudged open the door. The woman gasped in admiration, and Honey advanced coquettishly. Condor took one look, one sniff, and was smitten. The decision whether or not to breed him was never mine to make.

I'd never seen my dog so determined about anything. In a matter of moments he'd wooed, subdued, mounted, and mated Honey. The woman and I watched speechless at the ardor and the precision of the dogs' mating behavior. Condor made out perfectly without the least bit of coaching.

Honey's owner opened a bottle of champagne, and we toasted

the unborn puppies and their parents. After that we mated them again to be sure, and then I had to leave on my trip through the mangroves. The woman and I made arrangements to keep in touch by phone. Since I planned to cover this assignment in three stages, I would be back in Miami to see the puppies and take the pick of the litter.

Two weeks later a call assured me that Honey was pregnant. "She's got morning sickness," her owner chuckled. "And she mopes around all day." After two months the woman called again. "Seven puppies were born last night," she announced happily. "Three pure white males, three honey-colored females, and one black-and-tan. That's the runt. They're all fine."

"How w-wonderful!" I stammered. "Where in the world did *white* shepherds come from?"

"I don't know," replied the owner, "but they're precious. Fluffy fur, black noses and paws. They're not albinos. Any idea which one you want?"

"Heavens, no. Not yet. I'll have to wait until I see them." I was stalling. "I'll be down in about three weeks, and maybe I can decide then. Personality is as important to me as color or sex."

I debated long and hard over my choice. A white dog would be lovely but hard to keep clean in the woods. It would also be an odd combination with Condor's black-and-tan coloring. Besides these reasons, a white coat was a recessive gene in shepherds, so I could not breed such a dog in all good conscience. Tan was not so attractive, yet I did think a female would be easier for Condor to accept than a male. As for the black-and-tan, the woman had failed to mention its sex, but she'd said it was a runt. I didn't want that!

When I returned to Miami to continue my assignment, I was eager to see the puppies. Seven bundles of soft fur, blue eyes, appealing whimpers, and musky puppy perfume wiggled around the lawn. Honey kept careful vigilance. She let me near her treasures only after she had recognized Condor's scent on my clothes. But she resolutely and firmly kept the father away.

Tenderly I picked each puppy up, turned it over, and tickled the fat tummy. I checked the size of the paws, shape of the face, lay of the ears. The white males promised to be huge and placid with fur as soft as Angora kittens or snowshoe hares. The tan females were petite, perky, and squealy with attractive black muzzles and eyebrows. The black-and-tan runt turned out to be a small female. She lay listlessly in my lap. There was something peculiar about her—like a Mongoloid with thickened neck and protuberant eyes. I looked her over again and suddenly felt an enormous lump on her neck beside the throat. No wonder she looked strange. It must be a goiter or tumor. It might be obstructing her swallowing of food, thus causing her small size.

Quickly I pointed out the malformation to the owner. She grabbed the puppy, touched the lump, and ran for her car. "Stay here and watch the others," she begged. "I have to get her to a vet immediately! Oh, I had no idea."

"I think she's going to die," I said soberly as the woman backed out of the driveway. "The dog really looks sick."

When she returned a couple of hours later, the puppy was gone. "I left her there," she explained, sinking into a lawn chair. "She may make it. The vet said she'd probably been bitten or scratched by one of her littermates, and it got infected. She shaved off the fur, lanced and drained the abscess, and gave her antibiotics. Thanks so much for finding that. You may have saved the puppy's life!"

Amazingly I had, for the woman's next report by phone declared the puppy cured, active, gaining weight, and intelligent. "She's a little lady," was her description, "compared to the others."

Now I was anxious to see her, for Brother Job assured me that the best of the litter would be the black-and-tan, for it meant she carried most of Condor's genes. Also, he told me a female was important to Condor's adjustment toward a second dog. He'd been top dog too long. A female would be more acceptable to him than a male.

On my third and last trip to Miami I was ready to select my puppy and bring it home. After I had considered all the alternatives, it seemed easiest to drive down and back and not trust to air express. Besides, my friend Karl wanted one of Condor's puppies as a surprise for his son Ricky. I agreed to bring a tan female. The two puppies could keep each other company on the ride.

I was nervous, approaching the woman's home again. Just as when I'd chosen Condor, I knew I was in for a lifetime commitment. Would I make the right choice? Would it work out right?

All my apprehensions lifted as I watched the adorable black-and-tan romp toward me and Condor. He sniffed the puppy briefly, then turned to Honey. They nuzzled each other like an affectionate old couple. Yet Condor apparently had no inkling that these imps were his offspring or that he was about to become an instant father.

I picked up the two puppies that were going with us, kissed them, and carried them out to my truck. They looked so tiny inside the loaded camper. As we were driving away, I spied a discarded kitchen sink on a trash heap alongside the road. It was in good shape, so I stopped and heaved it into the back of the truck, too. I figured it would find a use at Thoreau II, fifteen hundred miles away.

That evening, as I played happily with the two pups, it suddenly came clear they were askitter with fleas! I already knew that Miami was struck with a springtime outbreak of fleas of terrible proportions. Fleas were *everywhere* and were now sucking the blood of these helpless creatures.

So my first duty that night as the new "grandpuppy" was to bathe the two butterballs with flea shampoo, after which I dried them and bundled them up in soft towels for the night.

We took off the next morning for a drive of five long days. At night I was bleary with puppy tending. Because the two slept peacefully on the bed of the camper all day, they were full of energy at night, when Condor and I were exhausted. Since no motel would have accepted me with three dogs, I tented out in state campsites. After the day's ten-hour drive came the chores of setting up camp, cooking, feeding Condor and the pups, cleaning the back of the truck of puppy poop, and walking the dogs until they were sleepy. The puppies woke up every four hours and had to be fed and freshly exercised again. I recall hurrying along a sand road in Georgia at 2:00 A.M. under an umbrella as the two pups tagged behind me. (Condor cowered in the tent.) Another night two frisky youngsters and I jogged through a moon-washed pine forest in North Carolina at 4:00 A.M. And on a third occasion we loped in circles around a campfire in Maryland at midnight.

In Virginia I stopped beside a truck weighing station to picnic. The three dogs and I sprawled under tall pines to escape a scorching sun while huge semis rolled in and out. Later, as I grabbed some sun, Condor and his offspring explored the woods. Suddenly a huge eighteen-wheeler eased into a spot next to me. Both puppies pranced confidently up to the behemoth machine and sniffed one gigantic tire. They looked so fragile beside the wheel, which could have flattened them like bedbugs. Both had squatted down to relieve themselves when a red-headed, tobacco-chewing driver swung out of the cab and frightened them away. That night I discovered that each dog had picked up several ticks in the woods. Supper and sleep were delayed as I jiggled the tenacious parasites off tender skin with a glowing cigarette butt, tweezers, and alcohol.

Once we crossed the New Jersey/New York state line the

At the dock with Condor and the new puppy, Chekika.

southern heat wave broke and was replaced by a chill downpour and dense fog. I reduced my speed on the New York Thruway as huge tractor trailer trucks whizzed by me, deluging our small pickup with roadside spray. The poor puppies peered through the camper window, whimpering in fright. The rain must have sounded like bullets ricocheting off the aluminum cap. Had there been room, I would have put Condor in back to steady the little dogs, but the kitchen sink took up all the spare room. Talk about everything including the kitchen sink!

Soon after our return to the Adirondacks Ricky and Karl showed up. The puppy was still a secret. For all Ricky knew, they were dropping by for a cup of coffee en route to climb a high peak.

I gave Ricky a hug, then beckoned him around to the back of my truck. "Guess what I have in here, Ricky?" I opened the truck tailgate and camper door. Condor leaped out, and the two puppies tumbled toward us. Ricky threw open his arms and caught them.

"Oh, they're so cute!" he exclaimed. "Are they Condor's pups?"

"Yes, Condor is their dad. They were born in Miami," I explained, "and I'm keeping *one.*" I pointed at the black-and-tan "runt," then glanced at Karl for confirmation. He nodded. "And *this one's* for you, Ricky, from your dad."

The boy's eyes grew as round as an owl's. "Oh, boy. Oh, boy. Oh, boy." He cheered. He lifted the puppy and cuddled her in his arms. Having lost his mother, Ricky seemed to crave someone or something to touch and hold. He was so happy with the puppy that he put her in a pack basket and went mountain climbing that afternoon. He named her Couch-sach-raga, after this high peak.

My pick of the litter I named Chekika. It's the name of a ferocious Seminole Indian chieftain who defended the Florida Keys from white invaders during the mid-1800s. I figured the puppy needed a name like that to hold her own with Condor, King of Birds.

To say Chekika adapted to cabin life is an understatement. From the time she set her paws at West of the Wind she not only took everything in stride but took over! Her first evening in my home was a night of heavy thunderstorms, hail, and wind. My barometer hit 29.7—almost the lowest mark ever. This same storm killed seventy-eight or more people in Ohio, western Pennsylvania, and southern Ontario. Chekika was not in the least fazed. In fact, at the height of the tempest she chewed the wire from my CB radio set in half. If there'd been an emergency, it would have been impossible to make a call out.

She followed this prank by severing Mapuche's tail from his pelt as it hung by my desk. Then she shredded my paper birch wastebasket, disemboweled a number of pillows, masticated moccasins, gnawed holes in my Navaho rugs, and lacerated the llama fur piece. These were only her *indoor* escapades. *Outdoors* she devoured petunias, chewed charcoal, chased toads, leaped at dragonflies, rolled in deer droppings, and mouthed mushrooms. On one occasion, when I was splitting wood, she idled past, wagged her tail, and narrowly missed getting the end chopped off with a six-pound maul.

When Mike saw her, he knelt to pet her briefly, then said, "There goes your peace and quiet." He was right. 'Kika was more mischievous than Condor and Pitzi rolled into one. She spent hours dragging an old Ace bandage in front of Condor, hoping for a stretchy tug-of-war. On the trail she leaped alongside him, snapping at his ears and neck ruff. Eventually that poor male paced sedately behind me on the trail, seeking protection from the scamp. His ears were raw.

Since we were making daily trips through the woods to my new cabin site, I had to protect the older shepherd. A friend who raised bird dogs offered a solution. "Make a paste of Vicks' Vaporub and cayenne pepper," he advised, "and smear it on Condor's ears."

It worked. The first time 'Kika lunged for Condor's ears and got a mouthful of hot stuff, she spit and turned away. After trying to mutilate those ears several more times, she left Condor alone. However, she kept on chewing anything else that tasted OK, including his tail. I kept telling my big dog, "You'll like her once you get used to her."

Other friends were interested in the new puppy's develop-

Chekika, at three months, with her father, Condor.

ment. One day a package came by mail boat addressed to CHEKIKA, Black Bear Lake, Adirondack Park, N.Y. Inside were two pairs of little rawhide moccasins tied with pink ribbons—just for teething purposes. 'Kika demolished them in two days.

She took to Thoreau II amazingly well, too. At first I'd tried to carry her up in my pack, figuring a mile-and-a-half hike and paddle were too much for a three-month-old. She didn't like that one bit. Almost instinctively she found the trail and sniffed her way along gamely. When we got to the yellow canoe, she paused, then bravely put her front paws on the gunwale. Slowly the craft separated from the shore, and she stretched out like a sausage. Scrabbling madly, she clung with her paws to the canoe while her rear end sank up to the belly button. That was her rear half baptism in the world of water.

I didn't want Chekika to become frightened of canoes early in life, when she had years ahead to spend in them. So I dried her carefully with my shirt and set her gently inside the canoe near the stern. Then I knelt behind her in the paddling position. Pushing her into a sitting position, I tucked her little body between my thighs, head pointing toward the bow. That way she could see everything yet not bolt over the sides and tip us over. Condor leaped nimbly into the center of the canoe and sat down calmly. It seemed to help 'Kika to see him there.

Slowly I backed out of the tiny harbor and started up the pond. It was a still day, so the craft moved smoothly over the surface. 'Kika made two or three attempts to break free, but then she settled down. I kept stroking her head and praising her till we got to the end of the pond. Two more such rides, and she was "canoe-broken." (Today, weighing an even seventy-five pounds, just like Condor, she sits as quietly as he does and loves to go paddling. She's never tipped me over.)

It was also important to coax her into the motorboat. Getting in was all right, and everything was going well one morning as we raced down the lake with a load of garbage. The day was cold and blustery. As we tied up to the public dock, Chekika lunged to get out of the noisy, vibrating, spray-lashed boat. This time her front end plunged into the lake as she missed the dock! She plummeted down like a stone into seven feet of water. Luckily I was right beside her and immediately grabbed her neck and fished her out. I shudder to think what would have happened had she inhaled *underwater* from fright. In fact, I wasn't even sure that young puppies could swim. That was the front half of her baptism.

She proved she could swim on a rainy day when I carried two more big sheets of foil-lined R Max insulation to the new cabin. There was no room in the canoe, so I set Condor and 'Kika off on the trail. I knew they'd stay in full sight all the way around the pond. To my surprise, Condor abandoned the pup and raced ahead. She tried to follow him, lost his scent, and got scared. Hearing my voice from the canoe, she scrambled for the shoreline. I heard a big splash, and there she came, flailing toward me. Both ears were straight up and her legs thrashed in a dog paddle. Swiftly I approached her, but before I could reach the puppy, she encountered a bed of lily pads. She got tangled in the stems and splashed harder. I was terrified. Suddenly she broke free, headed back to shore, and dashed out, ears down, dripping wet. I relaxed and headed in to rescue her.

But Condor had come back, and now the two raced on. I paddled up the pond, but just as I entered the marshy part, where bog rosemary, sheep laurel, and grasses make an impenetrable mat, she leapfrogged into the dense vegetation. I heard a shriek, then silence. My first fear was that she'd fallen into a beaver hole or canal. Once again I shot for shore, knowing I could never penetrate the mat. The canoe almost bounced off it. I pictured myself slogging through and finding a limp body, then having to carry it home and bury it—all because of two silly sheets of insulation.

But 'Kika got on top of things as usual. She suddenly broke

free, swimming in earnest, quietly and flatly. When she came alongside the canoe, I lifted her into the canoe. She shivered mightily until we got to shore, where Condor was waiting. One look at his ears, she gave a leap, and they were off and running.

Since then any time I have bulky materials which fill the canoe, the two dogs swim. They refuse to take the trail, though they know it well by now. We make an odd flotilla—two pair of

The "flotilla." The two dogs swam behind me whenever I transported materials and there was no room for them in the canoe.

erect ears, two pair of bright eyes, and two snuffling snouts behind a yellow canoe with paddler.

At Thoreau II 'Kika is always underfoot. She never lets me out of her sight. During the building, when I climbed Ricky and Linda's makeshift ladder, she sat at the bottom chewing rungs. When I was on the roof nailing on steel, she lay right under the eaves, narrowly missing a squash from a sheet which slipped off. Even when I was chain sawing, she sat nearby, oblivious of the noise, quizzically watching the flying chips. Her ears moved like Morse code flags: both up, one sideways, both flat, then both the other side. Condor, on the other hand, curled up in a hollow yards away, enduring the noise with stoical calm.

Somehow, Chekika came through the construction phase unscathed. In certain respects, up to six months of age, she was certainly living up to her namesake—Chekika—ferocious warrior.

In disposition the two dogs are quite different. Chekika is extremely sensitive and affectionate. Whereas Condor will accept a scolding with equanimity, 'Kika is crestfallen for hours after one harsh word. And whereas Condor considers two licks and a nudge his pleasant greeting, Chekika smothers my face with "kisses" and will lie beside me for hours. She often belly-ups and lies spraddle-legged, in a most unladylike position, begging for tummy tickles.

Since I am speaking of one's becoming a lady, 'Kika reached puberty at seven months and two days, which seemed very precocious to me. Something I didn't know at the time, as she neared her first heat, was that her whole personality would change. She became withdrawn, stopped playing, barely ate, whined softly, and generally disregarded me. First I was afraid she was sick or had worms. I babied her, fixed special meals, gave her Bufferin. All to no avail. Baffled, I was about to take her to a vet when

---

Chekika, full grown.

Condor showed an increasing interest in her, sniffing and lick-
ing. Suddenly what was happening dawned on me.

As Chekika got more edgy and coquettish, Condor became
more ardent and bold. I had to laugh at the quick changes he had
undergone in the space of a few months, going from simply ignoring his newborn pups, to barely tolerating 'Kika, to being placed
on the defensive by her outrageous antics, to valuing her as a female and paying her court. It was a fascinating display of animal
behavior, and it pointed up the strategic influence of sex hor-
mones in the lives of warm-blooded animals.

I wasn't interested in an incestuous relationship between
Chekika and Condor or in letting my puppy risk early parenthood,
so I packed Condor off to a friend's house. Then 'Kika and I settled down at my cabin to wait out the age-old feminine cycle.

After it was all over and Condor was reinstated at West of the
Wind, he was clearly in charge again. His maleness was affirmed.
His seniority and his wisdom all came to the fore.

Most of all, his close association with *me*, seen in their eyes as
the alpha wolf, or leader of our particular pack, gave him a high
status. Chekika was placed into a subdominant role (or a beta
wolf) farther down in the hierarchy. She now defers to Condor at
his food dish, water bucket, and sleeping mat. She lets him greet
me first in the morning and take his favorite spot in the front seat
of the truck. I also cater to Condor as top dog by feeding him first,
petting him ahead of 'Kika, and letting him in the house first.
After all, he's been my teammate for seven years and deserves the
best.

Somehow I sense Chekika doesn't mind. She and I have our
own special affection and closeness just as females do all over the
world.

14

A Copycat Walden

The heart of a cabin in the woods is its stove or fireplace. Its fire is the heartbeat, the life throb, which makes existence possible in these cold climes. Thoreau managed with a brick fireplace in his cabin, whereas I use an old potbellied stove in mine.

Mary gave me the stove when she moved. It was part cast iron, part steel, stood about four feet high, and weighed close to sixty pounds. The only way I could get it to Lilypad Lake was to wait till winter and toboggan it up through the snowy woods and over the ice-covered pond. This worked well. I left the stove smothered in plastic bags standing against a big spruce. A year and a half later, when I was ready to install the stove inside the cabin, it was intact, though somewhat rusty. One leg had cracked and would not support the stove's weight. Rod solved the problem by giving me four old firebricks to prop beneath. Snuggled in the bottom of my pack basket, they weighed thirty-two pounds. He hiked in with me to set the stove damper into a section of pipe and put the whole rig together. Installing stove pipes, like laying

The interior of Thoreau II, with my pot-bellied stove and quilt-covered rocking chair.

up rafters, is one of those cabin chores which demand two people to make it a success. Rod shoved the pipes through the hole in the wall and up in the air. We pushed on either end of the pipes until they were firmly together and the elbows on. I attached the cap and wired it securely to the cabin roof. We then nailed a sheet of asbestos against the inner wall to prevent possible fire.

It was time to try the stove out. Rod brought in some yellow birch bark curls and dry spruce branches, laid the fire, opened the damper, and struck a match. Within minutes a toasty warmth was radiating through the cabin while those shiny new stove pipes turned ashen gray in color as they "cured" from the heat. Everything worked fine, with a good draft. I dashed outside to see smoke rising above the roof and felt in my heart a glow as warm as the stove. Thoreau II was alive! And I could live there any time I wanted to.

In planning my furnishings, I decided to copy Thoreau's cottage at Walden Pond as far as was practical. My resolve was to take only essentials to the cabin, and certainly Thoreau was a master of economy. I made a list of the furniture and utensils he'd used and his general floor plan.

To begin with, the Walden cabin measured ten feet by fifteen feet, had a door, two windows, a closet, and a garret. There was a six-by-six-by-seven-foot root cellar for food storage. In contrast, Thoreau II was ten feet by ten feet, had two doors (screen and outer), two windows (main floor and loft), nails for hanging clothing, and a tiny loft. Instead of a root cellar, I carried in a large box of freeze-dried foods and other dry staples. I didn't want the slightest odor or taint of stored food to attract bears or raccoons. Both could ransack a place, but bears were positively destructive. If they caught the scent of something to eat, they usually broke into and entered a camp one way and exited another way, leaving large holes in the windows or doors. I'm not sure if black bears lived around Walden Pond in Massachusetts in the mid-1800s or if Thoreau faced a similar problem, but I felt justified in calling on this technological improvement over a root cellar.

As furniture and utensils, Thoreau included a bed, a table, a desk, three chairs, a looking glass three inches in diameter, a pair of tongs and andirons, a kettle, skillet, and frying pan, a dipper and washbowl, two knives and forks, three plates, one cup, one jug for oil, one for molasses, and a japanned (old-fashioned oil) lamp.

I deviated from Thoreau's plan by using a loft rather than a bed for sleeping, having my desk do double duty as an eating table, and using a stove rather than a fireplace with its attendant tools. Finally I treated myself to a *four*-inch mirror. I also carried in *three* knives, forks, spoons, and cups (why else have *three* plates?), a shiny metal pail for water, an old dipper, and kerosene in a plastic bottle. My only new purchases were a pail made in Mexico (cost: $2.89) and a pretty green glass kerosene lamp. There was no crockery jug for molasses, but there was a tin can with maple syrup.

Modern utensils not mentioned by the earlier woods dweller were a can opener, several cans of dog food, two dog dishes, two empty Grizzly Bear beer bottles and two Black Tower wine bottles for candleholders, and, of course, candles.

Thoreau had three chairs—"one for solitude, two for friendship, and three for society." That became my rule of thumb as well.

Two of my chairs were old dark oak folding types—from the pew of an abandoned chapel—which slipped under the desk. The third was a slender rocker set beside the stove. Thoreau also mentioned having paper, pens, books, and matches in Walden as well as a coffee mill. I had all the former, plus a typewriter, which I had purchased for $2.50 at the Salvation Army outlet store and carried in via a pack basket. I had no need for a coffee mill because my cabin was well stocked with cans of redolent Cuban espresso coffee obtained in Miami.

Other than his washbowl, Thoreau never discussed cleanliness in his book. Perhaps he was a dirty old bird with soiled underpants and cavities in his teeth. For my part, I've never felt comfortable being unkempt in the woods or in my cabin. So I brought an extensive list of items in this department. Besides the four-inch mirror, I had a comb, toothbrush, toothpaste, toilet paper, soap, skin cream, and towels. There was my old standby, the round horse-drinking tub which I used to bathe in outdoors on the porch during winter months at West of the Wind. I would fill it with buckets of hot water, scrunch myself in, cover my shoulders and head with a big poncho, and let the steam envelop me. Even when snow was falling, I kept warm and got clean. A broom, whisk

Two views of Thoreau's cottage at Walden Pond. He put his writing desk near the brick fireplace. *Photos by A. Edwards*

broom, liquid detergent, scouring pads, and dish mop completed the household cleansing inventory.

Another subject Thoreau never addressed was safety. He must have had the eyes of a lynx and the luck of an Irishman the way he wandered through the woods at night without any form of light. Some of his descriptions of returning home from town during storms are downright scary! I made sure to have flashlights and batteries in case of an emergency evacuation at night; a small transistor radio with batteries so I could hear weather reports; some first-aid gear, pain-killers, and an Ace bandage. Another safety measure was heavy wire nailed over the windows in the autumn to discourage bears and hunters from breaking in.

Perhaps the greatest difference between Thoreau and me in furnishing our cabins lay in the realm of aesthetics. While I was content to use nails as hooks for clothes and towels, rip planks out of logs for shelving, and attach an old wooden thread spool to the door as a handle, I did not intend to live without curtains, a rug, some bright cushions, colored candles, and a poster or two on the walls. The rug caused the whole room to blend with the outdoors. The design was called Stained Glass, a patchwork of muted greens, beiges, browns, and rusts separated by black lines. When I looked at it, I thought of spruce branches in silhouette against the lake and hills at twilight.

Friends marveled that I could live and function in a ten-foot-by-ten-foot building. But basically there was room for everything, and the room was streamlined. The narrow plywood desk (six feet by two feet) ran under the front windows with a beautiful view of Lilypad. It was the desk I had had since I began free-lancing twenty years before. The two chapel chairs slipped underneath the desk or folded against the wall. The sink I'd transported from Miami sat in one corner with the Mexican pail in the tub part and a two-burner gas Coleman stove on the flat section. (I wasn't going to cook on a campfire in sleet and snow.) Moreover, the sink

My writing desk, with its window view at Thoreau II, also serves as an eating table.

was a lovely avocado color which matched the rug. The rocker took up the center of the room and was covered with a cherished old Kentucky patchwork quilt. The potbellied stove stood against the north wall between rocker and desk with a woodpile beside it. (That being the coldest wall, it was the best place for the stove.) High shelves held numerous odds and ends. Since the cabin walls were seven feet high, I did not feel jammed in or overhung with gear.

The sleeping loft held two foam rubber pads (retired from my camping equipment), which ran the length of the windows, end to end. There were two sleeping bags, two pillows, and two red and white blankets. Red candles in the Black Tower bottles lent a cheerful touch and were sufficient for reading. Ricky and Linda's makeshift ladder gave access to the loft, provided one was part red squirrel.

My outhouse (something else Thoreau failed to mention in *Walden*) was made from three old long French doors, which a neighbor had given me years before. Through the glass panes on the upper part, I could gaze out at the forest, while the solid wooden lower section provided privacy. I used them as three sides of the building, with a gigantic yellow birch tree trunk as the fourth side and partial roof. I dug a hole deep among its roots, figuring that the wastes might act as fertilizer to the tree. Over the hole I set the plastic toilet housing I'd found in a deer hunters' camp. As at West of the Wind's outhouse, I used ashes from the stove to purify and deodorize excrement.

As the cabin neared completion in September, I began listing all the expenses and comparing them to what Thoreau had spent for his place 140 years before. Our purchases look like this: Thoreau spent $30.12 1/2; I spent $130.75, total.

Since we *both* used the free trees on our properties for the wood, probably the two biggest expenses for *both* of us were nails and spikes for building and stove or fireplace materials for warmth and cooking. There is just no other way to obtain metal materials such as stovepipes, damper, spikes, and so forth other than having a sheet metal worker or blacksmith as your good pal. And neither of these departments is a good place to skimp, for you don't want your cabin to fall down or burn up.

The other noteworthy difference in costs involved the state tax, the town building permit, and correspondence over Adirondack Park Agency regulations. None of these had existed in Thoreau's day. With what *I* paid out in state taxes for my purchases

Even the kitchen sink was transported to the cabin by canoe.

($7.77), *he* was able to build his brick fireplace! *My* local building permit cost more than all *his* boards. And although an APA permit was not necessary, I spent as much in postage back and forth as Thoreau spent in oil for eight months. So much for bureaucracy!

Finally, and sadly, there was my need for a hasp and padlock. Not too long ago in the Adirondacks (and, of course, in Thoreau's time), people could leave their camps unlocked, pack baskets standing in the woods, boats overturned on wild lakeshores. No one would enter or steal or damage anything. Today the threat of thievery and meddling from a few nasty hunters, hikers, or fishermen or from thoughtless teenagers makes it so that no one dares leave a house or boat unlocked, a backpack or pack basket unattended.

When I clicked shut the lock on the cabin door, I felt both safer and more nostalgic. The time for trusting one's fellow human being is fast passing. Thoreau wrote about finding visitors who had come in to his cabin and left their cards, "either a bunch of flowers, or a wreath of evergreen, or a name in pencil on a yellow walnut leaf or a chip." People were free to come and go. He never locked his door, even come evening. ". . . the black kernel of the night was never profaned by any human neighborhood." People invariably left "the world to darkness and to me."

I'm sure if I left *my* door open, half my gear would disappear during hunting season. At night I *always* lock the door, even with two German shepherds to guard me and a pistol under my pillow.

Whereas costs for the cabin were amazingly low, they really escalated in the *food* category. Thoreau reported living on twenty-seven cents a week! He was largely a vegetarian and grew most of his food, such as his famous beans, Indian corn, rye, a few peas, pumpkins, potatoes, and beets. He occasionally ate a mess of fish or a woodchuck. He also made a "satisfactory dinner" from a dish of purslane. His overall bill for an eight-month period was $8.74!

To all this culinary economy, I have only one reply: "Good for Thoreau, but it won't work for me."

In the first place, I'm not a vegetarian, and don't wish to be. Secondly, the soil has become too acidified, and my woods are too dense to farm successfully. Local fish have largely disappeared because of acid rain. Woodchucks are scarce in the wilderness. To hunt small or large game or waterfowl for food means buying licenses, adhering to set seasons, and obeying bag limits. Wild animals and birds are no longer available year-round, as they were when Thoreau lived. Many edible weeds do not grow in the dense Adirondack forests.

I can't begin to estimate what my food costs were at Thoreau II for a week, much less eight months. With a full freeze-dried dinner (main course, vegetable, and dessert) running about $8.00

for two; a jar of peanut butter around $1.95, and a can of espresso, $3.50, I'm sure I ate for $8.74 a *day*. Of course, I could do so for less, using canned goods, grains, rice, and water. Probably the only three items Thoreau and I would have had in common in our menus are salt, water, and molasses (though I substituted maple syrup). Even here I found a major discrepancy in prices. Thoreau spent three cents for an unspecified amount of salt (probably a pound), but it cost me twenty-five cents. His jug of molasses (no doubt a gallon) totaled $1.73, while maple syrup runs close to $25.00 a gallon.

All in all, it wasn't easy, or even advisable, to copy his cabin at Walden or to live like Thoreau completely. I didn't want to skimp on some of today's hi-tech gadgets that are so superior. For instance, I wouldn't give up my chain saw, aluminum canoe, canned dog food, manual typewriter, or fiberglass insulation in order to duplicate old-fashioned facsimiles or methods. I can give myself more time to write and explore, and I have more comfort than Thoreau did.

In summary, I found it was possible to build and furnish a tiny dwelling in the woods for about four times what it cost Thoreau 140 years ago.* (It meant cutting my own trees to do so, and this does *not* count buying and repairing a chain saw, transporting some materials by truck to my jumpoff point, or owning two canoes and paddles.) I discovered that good neighbors, willing friends, native ingenuity, and shrewd Yankee scrounging ability are still alive and well in the Northeast. What's come between a person's individual freedoms in the years between 1845 and 1985 is local and state bureaucracies, taxes, and laws. What's come

---

*Interestingly, copies of the most famous small house in American literature are getting costly. Roland Robbins, the man who discovered Thoreau's cabin, recently paid three thousand dollars for his reproduction. The Thoreau Society in Concord, Massachusetts, built a replica for four thousand dollars, and the state of Massachusetts paid seven thousand dollars for its in the summer of 1986.

Replica of Thoreau's cottage at Walden Pond. *Photo by A. Edwards*

My cabin at Lilypad Lake.

both to help and to hinder a person's wilderness life is high technology and all its gadgets.

Nevertheless, when I placed the key to Thoreau II on a length of rawhide and hung it around my neck, I felt a bond between my wee cabin and me as strong as between parents and their new offspring.

HENRY THOREAU'S EXPENSES

Boards (mostly shanty boards purchased from neighbor)	$8.03 1/2
Refuse shingles for roof, sides (from neighbor)	4.00
Laths	1.25
2 secondhand windows with glass	2.43
Door (probably made from boards)	—
1,000 old bricks	4.00
2 casks lime	2.40
Hair (?)	.31
Mantle-tree iron	.15
Nails	3.90
Chalk	.01
Hinges and screws	.14
Latch	.10
1 japanned lamp	?
1 washbowl and dipper	?
Transportation ("I carried a good part on my back")	1.40
	$28.12 1/2
Oil and some household utensils	2.00
	$30.12 1/2
State tax	—
Local building permit	—
Adirondack Park Agency permit	—
TOTAL	$30.12 1/2

Anne LaBastille's Expenses

17 one-by-eight-inch boards	
(scrounged from construction site)	$ .00
12 particle board sheets	
(scrounged from construction site)	.00
Plastic sheeting	3.99
4 secondhand glass windows (given by neighbors)	.00
2 secondhand doors (from neighbors)	.00
4 firebricks for stove (from Rod)	.00
1 potbellied stove (from Mary)	.00
Stovepipes, damper, cap	26.82
Asbestos wallboard	
(left over from West of the Wind)	.00
Nails and spikes	9.76
4 each two-by-fours and two-by-ones lumber	12.04
Hinges, hasp, padlock, hook	10.21
1 roll fiberglass insulation (for chinking)	12.77
1 chainsaw file	1.79
Steel roofing sheets (from dump)	.00
1 kerosene lamp	3.99
1 tin pail	2.89
1 sink (from trash pile in Miami)	.00
10 feet sink pipe, drain with plastic connector, ring	8.12
Roof paint	4.88
Transportation (I carried everything on my back)	.00
	$100.98
Oil, kerosene, chainsaw gas	10.00
	$110.98
State tax	7.77
Local building permit	10.00
Adirondack Park Agency permit (postage only)	2.00
TOTAL	$130.75

15

Sauntering Around
Lilypad Lake

I began living at Thoreau II during the harvest moon of September. Maroon maples cloaked the hills. Nights were chilly, but frost had not yet touched the land. At dawn Lilypad Lake was muffled with mists. As the sun rose behind Lilypad Mountain, the mist lifted in streamers until the water shone like a mirror. Day after day was warm and sunny. The swallows, swifts, hummingbirds, and warblers had headed south. Canada geese were still to come. It seemed a magical interlude between summer and autumn, and it was almost two years to the day since I'd started my wilderness cabin.

This fall was my season of fruition. I wanted to spend several days at Thoreau II writing, walking, and contemplating nature and enjoying a respite from all the intrusions, delays, injuries, demands, and frustrations of the past years. When I spoke to Mike about this, he was less than enthusiastic.

"What if you get hurt way back in there?" was his immediate

reaction. "No one would know. I can't be with you. Several big cases are pending over the next two weeks."

I knew my safety was foremost in the mind of this physician, (and rightly so), but somehow I'd expected and needed his encouragement. As before, when I'd moved into West of the Wind, I felt certain apprehensions about being alone so far from other humans.

"Why can't you write at your big cabin?" Mike went on. "Or better yet, come on down here early this year. You know I love to have you spend the winters with me. Why not the fall?"

He had missed the point entirely. "Two reasons," I tried to explain. "I want to savor Thoreau Two after all the time and headaches it's taken to build it. Secondly, I *need* to go there to write, *really write*, my book undisturbed. It's the same way you *have* to be in a hospital to work, not a shopping mall. Well, I *have* to be in the woods, not in town. Don't you see?"

He didn't; he couldn't; he wouldn't. There were too many differences between our respective professions. The conflict hung there unresolved. Yet I was determined to go. The words of Isaiah (54:2–3) came to mind and supported my decision: "Enlarge the place of thy tent, and let them stretch forth the curtains of thine habitations: spare not, lengthen thy cords, and strengthen thy stakes; for thou shalt break forth on the right hand and on the left. . . ."

Therefore, on a golden afternoon I made my preparations. Packing some perishable food, my pistol, books and notes, cameras and film, binoculars, and the dog whistle in a pack basket, I hiked up and settled in. Just before nightfall, I went down to the lake for a bucket of water and a look around. I felt somewhat forlorn. Yet I was in a far better state of mind than when I'd moved into West of the Wind. The years of working and living in the woods had strengthened my self-confidence and courage in ways that could never have happened in a city and with a city job. And my emotional attachment to a fine man had filled the lonesome corners of my heart.

Coming back up the knoll, I looked at the tiny cabin and gasped in surprise. The candles flickering on my desk cast a soft glow throughout the room. At the same time peach and cream reflections from the sunset shone on the narrow-paned windows. My retreat looked like a little shrine. I stood transfixed. Deep inside I knew I'd been right to come here.

Stepping carefully over the log sill so as not to spill water on the floor, I set the bucket inside the Miami sink. Then I filled a pan with water for the dogs and took several long swallows from my dipper. Finally I stood in the center of that room, letting the silence envelop me and the smell of new wood fill my nostrils. I could scarcely believe that the retreat was finished. I was so used to hauling, pounding, measuring, sawing that I hardly knew what to do with myself.

Then practical matters motivated me. The dogs were hungry. My stomach was rumbling, too. The cabin was cooling down. Sleeping bags had to be unrolled and fluffed up. All the normal cabin chores were waiting here. After everyone had been fed and the stove fire was crackling, I sank down in the rocker and threw the old patchwork quilt over my legs.

The next morning a young white-throated sparrow greeted me with an amusing rendition of the normal "Sam Peabody-Pea-body-Peabody" song. Like an adolescent choirboy whose voice is changing, this sparrow cracked on high notes, skipped some low ones, and chimed a whimsical new white-throated melody. An incandescence grew in the southeast as the sun rose. The pearly fog trembled, turned pinkish. A lone ruddy duck traced a smooth arrow on the platinum surface. 'Kika whined, and Condor thumped his foot on the floor in a morning scratch. Time to get up! I bounced down the ladder and was smothered with doggie licks, kisses, sideswipes, and tail wags. Time for a swim!

I knew that wading off the point would mean sinking into the slimy lake bottom. Yet like Thoreau, bathing in a pond every morning was practically "a religious exercise, and one of the best things which I did." I decided to enter from a rock by the beaver dam and outlet. I slipped in without a splash and swam toward the main lake with only my head out of water. Suddenly a brown head appeared around the little point, coming my way. The two dogs were quiet, watching from shore. I continued toward the animal, and it toward me. It was a small beaver. No doubt it had finished its night's feeding and was headed to its newly mudded lodge on Birch Pond.

At twenty feet away I could see its nose, whiskers, eyelashes, and perky short ears. Its eyes glinted brightly in the strengthening light. Beavers have fairly poor sight, and this one was no exception. It finally slowed down about fifteen feet away, sniffed, and turned sideways as if to watch better this beaverlike object sculling near its dam. I trod water. It stopped, slapped its tail hard, and dived. What a way to start the day.

Over Cuban espresso, bread and jam, I resolved to saunter around Lilypad Lake my first day at the cabin. Thoreau speaks of "sauntering" as the art of taking walks. (The word is derived from the Middle Ages, when idle people went to *Sainte Terre*, or the Holy Land.) A saunterer was a seeker of holy lands. Such walkers, says Thoreau, belong to a fourth estate, outside of those of church, state, and people. That's how I felt as I viewed the "fourth estate" stretched out before me—now clear and mirroring the burgundy-colored hills. I was free, unobtainable, detached from the other three estates, and open to adventure.

Heading east, I crossed the outlet of Lilypad Lake and descended through a tawny tangle of ostrich ferns. Rust, tan, and gold fronds nodded in the slight breeze. Individual leaflets were curled up from frost almost like the fertile fetal fiddleheads of spring seeking the sun. Crimson maple leaves had

Morning mist over
Lilypad Lake.

fallen on some horizontal fronds and lay like rubies on topaz.

I picked up a dim trail along the eastern lakeshore and moved easily through sunny hardwoods. Red squirrels chattered as we passed, and a pileated woodpecker tapped noisily on a yellow birch stub. Along the way, three marks made by humans caught my eye. One, a crumbling wooden sign pointed the way to a distant pond. It had been nailed up decades earlier. Then there was a shiny yellow and blue Department of Environmental Conservation metal poster, indicating I had crossed into a wilderness area. And lastly, a rusty tin can with a wire handle hung beside a nameless brook. Someone had drunk here years ago and left this simple dipper. I put it in my pack to hang on the cabin wall. It was a memento of the third estate, which it seemed I could not avoid.

Where the brook and trail turned to climb a hill, I left and sought the shore again. Plowing into the marsh that skirts Lilypad, I headed for a tiny "island" barely connected to land by watery tussocks of sedges. On its south side I stripped off my shirt and lay down on a warm, sunny rock. The dogs curled up on cool sphagnum moss.

We were not alone. Dozens upon dozens of dragonflies performed aerial maneuvers above the marsh. Their transparent wings glittered in the sunshine as whole squadrons zoomed straight ahead over the water as if in pursuit of something. Pairs circled, dodged, hovered, and locked together in embraces which still permitted them to fly straight or in circles. Lone dragonflies darted like miniature projectiles in all directions. The lake was alive with these insects.

As I sat watching and munching a Bartlett pear, one black-and-blue-striped fellow, long as a Tiparillo, lit on my hand. At first I thought he coveted my fruit, but then I saw his bottle green head and proboscis were busy mincing up a beetle he'd just captured. He devoured the entire insect as I watched, inches away, face-to-face. Snack over, he zipped off after new prey. Then it came to me. The dragonflies are the A-10s of the insect world: predatory, businesslike, noisy, but tactically brilliant. In fact, their motto could be the same as that of the Air National Guard jet fighter pilots who have disturbed the peace at Black Bear Lake: "Get Ugly Early."

Maybe there's little basic difference between insects and humans. One attacks prey directly to eat and survive; the other captures natural resources and the financial wealth of its victims.

As I was mulling over this observation, three new signs of humankind intruded. One was the noon whistle from the Hawk Hill fire hall, six crow-miles away, blown in by the south wind. Another was a silvery military jet spiraling fifty thousand feet in the air. And third was the distant drone of a helicopter. No doubt it was taking water samples for the state's acid rain survey.

Still another reminder of civilization met my eyes as I was dozing through the noon hour. Many dramatic-looking stumps and snags, long dead, rose around the tiny island. Some had been cut about four feet above the ground (or snow level), just like the ones at Birch Pond. Evidently the same lumberjack of winters past had come here to harvest his cabin posts of tamarack and rafters of spruce. I was not the first to cut trees on this land.

As I finished sunning, I saw that the rock beneath me was covered with curly brown lichens. I peeled some off, popped them in my mouth, and let them soak up saliva. When they were as chewy as cheese curds, I swallowed them. They were a cross among mushrooms, brewer's yeast, and consommé in taste. They *might* fill a hungry person up—if he or she were short of peanut butter sandwiches.

Lunch and lichens over, I continued to skirt the lake to its inlet. A brooklet entered from a swampy area above. Deciding to take a look at that, I entered a hemlock and balsam thicket. A blue jay rose, screaming alarm, and a minute later a ruffed grouse thundered away. Condor and Chekika scrambled after them.

Ahead of me I saw a new beaver pond with a perfect reflection of autumn trees. The animals had been busy, for a dam about five hundred feet long ponded up two acres of water. Scarlet and yellow leaves fell sporadically onto the placid surface. Their ends curled up like the tops of my two canoes. As the breeze blew erratically, they all first veered one way, then sailed slowly back toward me like a little brigade of voyageurs.

Back at the head of the lake I found a small sandy area and decided to swim. I took off the dogs' collars and my clothes, and we waded in. The bottom was not as slimy as on the other side, but still, clouds of muck billowed up under us. The sun was hot and the water refreshing as we dogpaddled around. Then the distant sound of a seaplane came to my ears.

I began to swim for shore, but the muck slowed me down. I'd barely reached the sand when a plane flew over the hill, veered, and headed straight toward me. There wasn't time to throw on a stitch, so I called the dogs, crouched down, and pulled them in close to me. The pilot flew directly overhead and waggled his wings. I hung my head and hoped he'd overlook the assortment of black, tan, and blond coloration below—but I doubt it. So much for sauntering in the nude!

Now I headed back along the steep north-facing slope under the brooding brow of Lilypad Mountain. The difference in microclimate was instantly noticeable. I felt as though I were climbing into a giant terrarium. The air was cool and damp on this shady slope. Each stone was blanketed with lush moss; every fallen log was a garden of partridgeberry, sphagnum, and baby hemlocks. The forest was as wild and untouched as any in the Adirondacks. Birches, three and four feet in diameter, soared against the blue September sky. Some of their roots spraddled rocks and formed crannies where a raccoon could easily hide. Huge hemlocks and spruces stood ramrod straight above a profusion of ferns.

I was elated to find this patch of primeval forest and grateful

that it could never be cut. While I agree that so
harvested like crops—be it corn or cotton
think all of them should be considered crops.
too many clear-cuts, shelterwoods, and selective lo
seen the berry bushes and pioneer trees slowly fill in
Although regeneration over decades will heal the scars, mos
bered sites look and are ravaged. The trade-offs—whether in pulp,
paper, veneer, furniture, or firewood—can never quite atone for
lumbering a virgin tract of trees. Sheer aesthetics, high-quality
water, and ecological balance are often more precious to maintain.

It also grieves me every time I see discarded newspapers blowing down city streets or stacks of paper plates and cups in the
garbage. These items were once trees. To have the forest I was
sauntering through come to such an end would have been infi-
nitely saddening.

The sound of water gurgling down the slope reached my ears.
On investigation, I found a whole series of crystal-clear rivulets,
half aboveground, half under, flowing downhill. Under the root
system of a fallen giant I found what I'd been hoping for: a spring
hole. Now I could come by canoe to fill jugs with icy, clean water
rather than use the lake or outlet. I stopped to move some stones
and deepen the spring hole.

Chickadees and juncos flitted and chattered in the balsams.
As I worked and the dogs rested, a young mink scampered along
the shoreline. When it caught our scent, it hissed angrily. Poised
and unfrightened, he did an agitated little tap dance atop a rock
at the sight of us. The youngster was still a fuzzy charcoal color
rather than the sleek mahogany of an adult. As the mink saw Condor rise, it thought better of it and slithered into a labyrinth of
tiny tunnels.

The slope steepened, and a rock face began. Gradually it
heightened and flattened until I reached a place where a cliff rose
twenty-five feet. The side was slick with moisture and moss, glis-

·ning like green Vaseline. Tiny trickles of water dripped tirelessly onto an emerald blanket of sphagnum at its base. The sun was all but blocked out. I shivered. This could be a spooky place on a rainy, windy night. But the brilliant blaze of an orange maple overhanging the cliff and a few lances of sunlight dispelled my quivers. I felt that I'd penetrated deep into the private root zone of Adirondack rock.

Stumbling through the narrow gully, I came face-to-face with an ancient blaze and trace of a trail. Could this be part of the old route those early hikers had followed to feast on homemade pies and tea at Black Bear Lake? It headed in the general direction of Thoreau II, so we took it. Witch hobble had grown up luxuriantly along the way. I pushed past leaves as large as pie plates, colored in enchanting shades of pink, lime green, vermilion, chartreuse, oxblood, olive, and magenta.

To my surprise, I came upon the same outlaw camp that had supplied my plates and cups for the cabin—how long ago? Bits of black plastic were still plastered to the ground. I ripped them up and found four frying pans. I'd overlooked them before, and surely this was proof that no one had been here for eight years. One pan was Teflon and in good shape. Another was stainless steel which folded in half for boiling or lay flat for frying.

The pans immediately came into use. Condor and 'Kika were ravenous after the long bushwhack, so I prepared their supper in the big Teflon one. Carrots and beets went in the other to boil for my supper.

As we all ate, the sky was slowly glazing over with silver and the fitful south wind was dying. Afterward I slid the canoe into the water, loaded the dogs, and began to circle the lake in the direction opposite to my earlier saunter. As I paddled, water bugs that had been invisible on the lake surface sprang alive and zigzagged away from me. Each one sparkled like a sequin. At least *they* throve on the acidic conditions. Wave after wave swarmed ever farther away. No wonder certain ducks and mergansers could survive here, at least temporarily, on this abundant food supply. A few fragile midges hung in the still air. Others lay dead on the water. More duck food.

I reached the standing dead trees and paddled among them as through a watery petrified forest. The low September sun hung above the far shore. In its slanted rays, every furrow, crack, jagged edge, and knot stood out on the snags like sculptured pewter. Under the standing trees their fallen limbs lay intact, pickled (it seemed) in the clear acidified water. The sun set. A lemon back-wash was left in the sky. One star stood out overhead. A stray robin sang its woodnote sleepily from shore. Wood toads began their evening chirping. A lone bat skimmed the surface for fallen bugs. Each time it snared one there was a tiny noise like a ciga-rette falling into the water—zifffft.

The lake was cloaked in austere purple and seemed larger than by day. In the last light a pair of hooded mergansers whirred down from the silvery sky and parted the water neatly in a long V for their night's rest. As I turned toward Thoreau II, both dogs were asleep in the bottom of the canoe, snoring gently. When I pulled up on shore, they woke and leaped out. The only sound now was the outlet faintly purling over the beaver dam.

Then from far off came the honking of geese. The first of the season! They were high and traveling fast. As always, tears spilled from my eyes at the thought of facing winter and all the dangers which lay ahead for those gallant birds until they rested for the season. I felt my arms beating like their wings, air rushing through the pinions. I saw the lakes, burgundy and black below their tired breasts. I willed them to turn toward my retreat and settle on Lilypad for the night. I yearned to hear them "lumbering in the dark with a clangor and awhistling of wings," as Thoreau had when they came into Walden Pond. But they moved on. Others would come and find refuge here. I turned to the cabin and went in.

Later in my loft I thought back on the day. If this was sauntering—by foot or by paddle—then truly I'd spent a day in *Sainte Terre*—my holy land. As I fell asleep, the constellation Cassiopeia crept through a cleft among the conifers and gazed calmly down upon the cabin.

16

Neighbors

While I was eager to leave the hustle and bustle of Black Bear Lake for the tranquillity of Lilypad, I had no wish to abandon all society. Neither did Thoreau. He made his daily or weekly trip to town for supplies, selling his garden produce, or visiting friends. Likewise, I have neighbors at Black Bear Lake and nearby Hawk Hill whom I love to see and with whom I have close bonds. Partly it's because we live in an isolated location, share a woodsy life-style, and enjoy beautiful scenery. Everyone who owns a camp here must reach it by boat, and most property lines border on a state wilderness tract. More important, we care about one another up here. Whether one comes to a camp only on Fourth of July and Labor Day or stays all summer and fall, this pioneer ethic predominates. It's one of the reasons I insist on living here, not in a city where I'd feel anonymous.

The couple who operated the mail boat for several summers were unusual neighbors. Their camp was about a quarter of a mile back from the lakeshore. Although accessible only by trail, it was not nearly as remote and difficult to reach as Thoreau II. Nevertheless, getting there was a stout hike for a man and woman in their seventies, since everything had to be carried in and out by pack basket. This included groceries, twelve-volt batteries, kerosene, and coal.

Each morning Millie and Stu would get in their motorboat, cruise slowly around the lake to pick up the outgoing mail, go to the public landing to meet the mail truck at the end of its run, load the incoming mailbags in their boat, and deliver them individually to our docks.

Mailtime was a big event in most camp owners' lives. It certainly was for me and my dogs. In spite of a strict U.S. postal schedule, Stu always took the time to share a few news items while he let his motor idle and adjusted his black beret. And Millie usually had some new merchandise in her collection of home products for sale. She was a sales representative for a natural vitamins company, a household cleanser line, and a national brand of cosmetics. She used all the products herself and swore by them. Judged by her spryness, facial makeup, and charm, not to mention her tidy cabin, the products worked well.

I often visited Millie and Stu in late afternoon, especially if they needed help toting coal to their camp. Years before, a former owner had brought a heavy coal-burning stove to that camp by horse team and installed it. Stu found it easier to carry in coal than to cut down trees, split logs, and stack firewood. However, he always laid up a cord or two of wood for the fireplace during the fall.

I'd go down by boat with my pack basket and fill it from the heap of black nuggets by the shore. Then I'd trudge up to their camp, dump the coal, and relax on the porch awhile. Millie always served cold orange juice. Stu always smoked his pipe. The roof eaves were hung with flowery red hummingbird feeders, so the porch was alive with these iridescent emerald birds. Jetting in from the forest, they'd flit from feeder to feeder, sipping sugar water. Sometimes there were young learning the ropes and waiting for their elders to assuage their hunger. They'd hover helicopter fashion until a feeder was free, then take a turn. They had a hierarchy as well defined as a wolf pack. The hummers thought nothing of zooming within inches of Millie's carefully combed hair or the glowing embers of Stu's pipe. These tiny birds were a source of endless entertainment.

As dark approached, we might move indoors and sit in front of the flickering stone fireplace while we gossiped. Brightly colored Navaho rugs lay scattered on the well-waxed floor. Kerosene lanterns glowed in corners of the yellow birch-paneled room. A battery-operated tape deck played old-fashioned waltzes. There was even a TV (operated by battery) in case a good show was desired. Stu and Millie had created an aura of rustic elegance.

Twice a year the couple drove to California, leaving right after the mail boat contract expired in September and returning just before it began in June. They spent a week driving each way, crisscrossing the country by various routes. Out in California, they'd keep busy visiting various grandchildren, playing in a kitchen band with other septuagenarians and octogenarians, restocking their home products, and carrying on an extensive correspondence with other camp owners at Black Bear Lake. Since no one except for two retired men, lives year-round at Black Bear Lake, people try to keep in touch over the long winters. This is where their hearts are.

Even after Stu had died at the age of eighty, Millie kept coming to Black Bear Lake, although she gave up the mail boat run. Because of heart trouble, she stopped driving cross-country and flew instead. Finally, in her eighty-second year, Millie concluded that the trek into her camp was too grueling. She decided to stay in California but pined for the Adirondacks. The regulars—six to eight property owners who stay at Black Bear Lake six months of the year—all invited Millie to stay at their camps. So did I.

Millie returned to Black Bear Lake once, for one day. All

those who loved her congregated on their docks to greet the mail boat when it came around with its honored passenger. We had gifts, hugs, invitations, and good wishes for Millie. That was the last time we saw her.

The mail boat route was taken over by a younger neighbor. Rusty is a cheerful, no-nonsense woman in her forties who is as strong as a spruce. She whizzes up and down the lake, red hair tousled by wind and rain, with her white dog and youngest child in tow. Rusty runs a businesslike postal schedule, seldom stopping to chat. But she's always ready to return on her own time to lend a helping hand if someone needs it. Over the years she's helped me manhandle two-hundred-pound propane tanks into place, delivered lumber and medicine, and warned me of possible intruders. Like Millie, Rusty carries a few items in her boat for sale. She specializes in T-shirts and sweatshirts with Adirondack logos. She also willingly passes out notices of property owners' meetings and the annual Neighbor's Day picnic.

Perhaps someday the mail boat will take on all the characteristics and services of the old "pickle boats" which once plied many Adirondack lakes inaccessible by road. These boats used to deliver mail and newspapers and also brought fresh milk and butter, sold a few groceries (including dill pickles), and transported guests and sightseers. Black Bear Lake may be too small and underpopulated for such a luxury; however, there'll always be a need for a community network of news and mail.

My favorite neighbors live across the lake from West of the Wind and are the ones who keep my phone machine. Sally and Sid love Black Bear Lake as much as I do. Although their regular house isn't too far away (by mountain standards) and very comfortable, they spend every day they can at their camp from ice-out to ice-in. Sid is retired but has dozens of projects going on around his property, including cutting wood and growing a garden. In fall he hunts daily with his cronies.

Aside from the obvious usefulness of knowing neighbors who have electricity and a phone line, Sally and Sid are the souls of hospitality. Our "coffee hours" are often the highlight and respite of my working days. It's not just the food we share but the caring and teasing and rejoicing over little problems and joys.

In a wilderness setting, neighborly concerns often loom large. There is the matter of hair care. The closest beautician and barber are about thirty-five miles away, so Sally trims my bangs and split ends (she cuts Sid's hair, too). She has lovely champagne-colored, curly hair, and I sometimes help her choose a new hair rinse or hairstyle.

There's also the matter of tools and building materials. One of us is always fixing or building something. Sid and I lend or give equipment back and forth to save the fifty-mile round trip to a hardware store. Sid is a master mechanic and often advises me on the proper way to run my various engines.

My two neighbors often urge me to pop over if I need a therapeutic hot shower or want to watch "Dallas" on color TV. While I can't repay this generosity in kind, sometimes I'm able to offer some useful advice or solace. Once Sally was sick during the summer and dreaded making the long trip out to see an internist. I decided to practice a little "bush medicine." I brought my *Merck Manual* and *Physicians Desk Reference* to her kitchen, and we researched her symptoms over coffee. I found her ailment and the remedy. Then, to be sure, I called Mike and checked it out with him. He concurred with my diagnosis and sent word to the local pharmacy for a prescription. I drove down to pick it up. When Mike came to visit me that weekend, he double-checked on Sally's condition and found her already halfway cured.

Another time Sid lost his dog. He had two beautiful beagles and used them in hunting trials every fall and winter. The dogs stayed in open kennels behind the camp and were allowed to run free each evening. Apparently a marauding black bear smelled the beagles. It must have stealthily analyzed the situation and then lain in wait. The young female dog took off on the trail of a snowshoe hare one evening and ran into the bear.

Later Sid whistled and whistled for the dogs, but only the male returned. The next morning Sid began a search and found small pawprints beside the larger ones of a bear. Then there was a spot of blood and a tuft of hair. The bear's tracks went straight up a mountain, into a dense alder swamp, and disappeared. Sid, who could go no farther, was sure that the animal had carried the beagle's body into the swamp and devoured her. As a dog lover I readily sympathized with the anguish he felt.

A few weeks later Sid got his revenge. A big bear had been sneaking around his woodshed and toolhouse at night, trying to open an old refrigerator where Sally kept soft drinks and extra frozen food. Two or three mornings the couple had found the big white box moved slightly. Only a bear was strong enough to do this. Sid stayed up one night, waiting at a second-story window with a loaded shotgun. He devised a string trigger which would ring a tiny bell if the bear entered the woodshed. At 4:00 A.M. the bell tinkled. Sid jerked wide-awake from a doze, flicked on a spotlight, and shot the bear in the back of the head. While he'd never know for sure if it was the same one that killed his beagle, he found it was large enough and aged enough to be taking some "easy meat."

Perhaps it is serendipitous that Sid has been my only unexpected visitor at Thoreau II. During the first fall, when I went to my retreat to write, saunter, and reflect, a storm raged one night. The next morning, as I was making espresso and poking in the potbellied stove, I heard a shrill blast from a dog whistle. I dashed out the door with both dogs in pursuit.

There came Sid with his deer rifle, plaid hunting jacket, and old red cap, searching out my dim trail. He had no idea where the cabin stood; he only knew that I had been building something at the back of my property near Lilypad Lake. By blowing his whistle, he was letting me know he was in the woods and looking for me.

Rushing up to him, I exclaimed "What a great surprise! How did you ever find me?" We embraced, and I said, "You're in time for coffee—come on in."

Sid's powerful frame practically filled the cabin, and the small rocker creaked as he sat down. The ten-by-ten-foot room suddenly seemed minuscule and fragile now that it contained another human being. Sid beamed as he looked around. He had the good sense not to try climbing Ricky's makeshift ladder to see the loft. "I like it," he announced. "But it sure is way back in the woods. Sally and I were worried about you last night, so I decided to check up on you. Oh, and here's some freshly baked banana bread she sent you."

As I sat smiling at him, there was a small lump in my throat. The first visitor to my retreat had turned out to be the most neighborly of neighbors.

17

A Wild Winter at West of the Wind

After twenty years in the Adirondacks I am a great respecter of winter. In the mountains it takes a lot of preparation, logistically and physically, to be ready for it. After my idyllic September days at Thoreau II I had to get West of the Wind squared away, then complete other winter chores at the new cabin. Though I knew I would be away on assignments for a good part of the coldest weather, in and out of airports, and near Mike, I wanted to stay at my cabins at any and every opportunity. So I laid up piles of firewood at Thoreau II, tacked extra insulation around the sleeping loft, and stapled plastic over the outer log walls. I also put stout posts under the roof as extra supports against the snow load. I hadn't seen Lilypad in winter's grip since two years before, when I had towed my stove up by toboggan. But I knew that the snows would be deeper, and the temperatures lower, at Lilypad Lake than at Black Bear Lake. The land was higher, for one thing. In addition, the new cabin would be harder to heat since the logs are smaller there and the roof is not insulated. So I prepared for the worst of winter, in part because of my condition.

I am becoming a chionophobe—a Greek word for one who dislikes cold. There's something else. I find it harder and harder to tolerate snow and ice. It has to do with my hands. After years of chain sawing, hammering, chopping, hauling, shoveling, and doing other heavy woods work, I've developed Raynaud's disease, or white fingers. As soon as my hands get cold—whether from frigid water, chopping ice, or making snowballs—my fingers start to tingle, become numb, turn bone white, and ache. Many lumberjacks, stonemasons, carpenters, and seamstresses develop this disability over time. Basically it starts when the main nerves to the hands swell from repeated trauma and cause small blood vessels to spasm. But since the nerves must pass through a narrow tunnel amid the small wristbones, the nerves are pinched, and the fingers suffer. As soon as the hands are warmed, the symptoms go away, usually in about twenty minutes.

Yet each winter I found I was spending more and more time with those white fingers stuffed in my armpits or soaking my forearms in buckets of hot water, then smearing them with Icy Hot or Ben-Gay. There was relief, but only for a little while. Each winter things got worse. It was often agonizing to go snowmobiling, or cross-country skiing, or snowshoeing on supercold days. So I just stayed indoors and felt like a hothouse flower.

Eventually Mike did some tests and told me about a simple operation that might reverse the situation. It was called a carpal tunnel. He would enlarge the little tunnel (through the wrist's carpal bones) and give the nerves more room to swell if they were still being abused (as mine were and probably always will be).

To submit to surgery was, for me, like lying down to die. Steadfastly I tried to delay it, but when too many nights of sleep had been broken by throbbing hands, the need for aspirins and hot-water bottles, I gave in. Besides, I hoped the operation would allow me to participate in the rest of winter, not avoid it.

When I checked into the day surgery unit at the hospital, I felt as if I were going to the guillotine. The thought of being put to sleep and out of control was terrifying. I'm sure I gave the admitting nurse a hard time. I'm sure I stalled getting out of my clothes and into the greens. I'm sure I shuddered when I was asked to lie down on the ice-marble operating table under the glaring lights.

And then Mike walked in, as nonchalantly as if he were picking up a pizza at a fast-food stand. He smiled and gave me a wink as he pulled on sterile gloves. "Everything's going to be fine, sweetie pie," he said reassuringly.

A nurse tied a mask over his face and adjusted the cocky green surgeon's cap he always wore. Then his steady gray-green eyes

Laying up wood for winter at Thoreau II.

were boring into mine, shining with love and concern. He stood over me and inspected my wrist. The anesthetist was bearing down with his needle and IV. I felt a prick in my arm. "One hundred, ninety-nine, ninety-eight . . ."

Two hours later I awoke in the recovery room, my right hand and arm bandaged to the size of a horse's hoof and leg. I felt woozy but fine, especially after Mike had ducked in for a moment to make sure everything was going the way it should.

"Everything went fine," he said, "but you swore in your sleep. . . . You shouldn't have any trouble this winter now. See you this evening, honey."

When the wooziness left me, I sat up, determined to leave the recovery room as soon as possible. Mike had arranged transportation for me back to his camp since hospital regulations forbade a patient recently under anesthetic from driving alone. After a light lunch and a snooze I felt ready to go outdoors. Bundling up like an Eskimo, I walked to a nearby lake and strolled out on the ice to watch ice fishermen setting their tip-ups and catching fish. Two weeks later my right hand seemed 90 percent better. That carpal tunnel operation gave me a new lease on winter life in the Adirondacks. I hoped it would stand up to roughing it at Thoreau II.

My first excursion to the cabins came after Christmas. It was a mild day. I had boxes of books for West of the Wind and canned food for the smaller cabin. My toboggan was well loaded and secured with stretch cords. The roads had been clear all the way to Black Bear Lake, and the forecast was for overcast skies but temperatures remaining warm. I reckoned this was a lucky break, for I'd seen storms that had dumped two feet of snow and raged for three days at this time of year.

As soon as I left my truck and strapped on snowshoes, however, I could see trouble ahead. The lake ice was thick enough— an ax hole showed eight inches—but the thaw had left two inches of water standing on the surface. No way could I slog over that, pulling a toboggan on snowshoes. I'd have to plow through the woods. The first quarter of a mile was fairly easy as I found an old snowmobile track to follow. It gave good purchase over two feet of snow on the level. But once that ended and I started out over an unbroken surface, I sank half a foot with every step. And every time I raised a snowshoe, ten pounds of mush clung to it. Yet without the snowshoes, I went in up to my knees. The poor dogs had it even worse, plunging belly-deep with each paw step. That snow was the consistency of mashed potatoes!

It was now 3 o'clock. I knew it would be pitch-dark by 4:30 or 5:00 P.M. this time of year. I'd figured on an hour, an hour and a half at most, to make it to West of the Wind. It had never taken me longer than that. In fact, eighty-six minutes was the record, and that was after a blizzard had dumped twenty-eight inches of snow over the lake ice. But this trip was going to break the record —and my back!

Every few steps I had to bang the snow clots off the webbing of my snowshoes with a walking stick. The rawhide straps grew wet and began to stretch; I had to tighten them several times. The toboggan dragged sluggishly on the clotted-cream surface, tilting right and left. There is no trail to my place, and bushwhacking is over uneven land and through dense wood. The boxes of books and supplies tipped over a number of times and had to be salvaged. I was sweating heavily and stripped down to shirtsleeves. As I passed one summer cottage, I spied an outdoor thermometer. It read forty-five degrees Fahrenheit. Where I had to drag the sled across brooks, water had puddled. Soon my rubber packs, pants, boxes, and the dogs were soaked.

Four o'clock. I was less than halfway to my cabin. The constant strain on my arms was taking its toll. Like a reminder of the past, my fingers began tingling. As the light dwindled and the temperature dropped, a gray, ghostly fog curled up from the drowned lake. I stopped, burrowed in a box for the big spotlight I always carry, and set it atop the load for easy access. Now I was glad I'd made an extra stop for a fresh six-volt battery before leaving town. The old battery had been growing dim. It seemed prudent to have a backup, even though I never imagined having to use it in the woods.

The fog thickened and coiled among the fir trees. I tried to go faster, to take a shortcut, but ended by overturning my load once again onto the mayonnaiselike snow. When it was finally righted, I could find no vestige of an opening before me, only impenetrable balsam thickets. Reaching for the spotlight, I struggled ahead, trying to go uphill. By 5:00 P.M. it was fully dark and the light was played out. I unscrewed the nuts that hold the headlight to the battery. Taking off the old one, I tried to attach the new.

But one terminal would not fit into the hole of the lantern head. I sat down on the toboggan while the dogs dropped into the snow and panted nearby. No matter how hard I tried, the battery would not slip on. Grabbing my ax, I tried knocking the terminals sideways because I figured they had been damaged in shipping and were bent enough to miss the holes. In the dark it was like trying to hit a piñata blindfolded. No luck.

There I was, still half a mile from home, with no light, with no trail, bone-weary, with two hungry dogs and an obstinate toboggan. A thin thread of fear curled in my chest. Without a light I had only two choices. One was to head downhill till I came to the lake and take my chances on the watery ice. But if I hit a rotten section, I might plunge through and drown.

The other choice was to abandon the toboggan until morning and try to ferret my way through the forest. Maybe I could find the power line and see the skyline down its narrow right-of-way. As it skirted the shoreline a few hundred yards back, the line would lead me somewhere behind West of the Wind. I decided on that course of action.

As I unstrapped my backpack, which held food and my wallet,

I remembered that there was a small disposable flashlight in one pocket. It had been a spare during canoe camping the past summer, yet it still worked. The light lasted for about twenty minutes, then went dead. But at least it had taken us to the power line. With the fog so dense I could not catch any tree silhouettes. I was less than a third of a mile from my cabin but completely lost. Condor whined with exasperation and pawed the snow. He wanted his dinner. It was six o'clock.

Then I realized *he* knew exactly where he was and could see in the dark far better than I could. No wonder he was impatient. So I knocked the mashed potatoes from my snowshoes for the three hundredth time and followed the dogs. In thirty minutes we were at the back door of West of the Wind, trembling with fatigue and hunger. No homecoming had ever felt better than that evening with the Franklin stove crackling, the steak sizzling, and the Alpo cans opening. (Of course, I shared some steak with my guide dogs.)

The next day I retrieved the toboggan after more laborious tugging and some disconcerting hand tingling. Given that reminder of white fingers syndrome and the weather, I gave up plans to restock Thoreau II and simply snowshoed up to see the cabin for five minutes. All was well, but I felt sad not to stay there. Next trip!

When I returned to town, I took the faulty battery back to the store for exchange. I was still subdued by the strenuous and scary trip. Putting the battery on the counter, I asked a salesman how they could have sold a damaged product.

"There's nothing wrong with it," he said politely. "It's a brand-new twelve-volt battery."

"Twelve volt?" I asked indignantly. "My flashlight takes a six! Here it is. The terminals of the new one just won't fit the holes."

"Of course not," the salesman replied. "You should have been given a six-volt." He shrugged. "Sorry for the mix-up. The clerk must have been in a hurry. We keep the two boxes of twelves and sixes side by side, and they look a lot alike. But there's no way a twelve will fit that flashlight mount. Good thing, too. You'd really get sparks and burn out your light if you put them together."

I remembered whacking the terminals with the ax in a vain attempt to make the battery fit. How lucky it hadn't. All I'd have needed was to have a flashlight explode deep in the woods.

By now the manager had ambled up, noting our animated conversation. "Anything wrong?" he asked pleasantly.

"Oh, no, nothing much," I retorted. "Just a small mistake. It could conceivably have cost my life. . . ." I proceeded to tell the full story. By the time I was done, the whole store was abuzz. Suddenly I achieved notoriety and a new, free battery. Ever after, when I shop at this store, someone will chuckle and ask me if I need a twelve-volt battery.

My next trip to Thoreau II was in February. Heavy snows had fallen, and I was worried about the roofs. Mike decided to go with me and help shovel since he had a free weekend. This time Black Bear Lake was firm and hard-packed with two and a half feet of ice beneath its windblown surface. We skied up in about forty-five minutes with the toboggan in tow. Because of the white fingers problem, I'd sold my snowmobile the year before. It was too hard to start and too cold to ride. Besides, cross-country skiing is more pleasant, warmer, and safer. There is no way of getting your skis stuck in soggy ice as there is with a snowmobile. It is also my contention that ice conditions have changed a great deal on Black Bear and other lakes because of acid rain. There are many more days when the ice seems mushy, cloudy, and poorly formed—not clear, blue, and solid as in former winters. Perhaps the weather patterns are different, or perhaps it's the high acidity content of the water. At any rate, snowmobiles are now often entrapped in the mess and have to be chopped out and towed away.

When we reached West of the Wind, we were astonished by

the amount of snow. Although it was not Mike's first winter trip, he'd never been there after blizzards. A layer at least three feet deep smothered the roof. And where earlier loads had slid off, they'd created a complete snowslide from ground to ridge! After lunch we began the tedious chore of shoveling. The snow was so compressed by its own weight and several thaws that we had to make three downward jabs with the shovel in a box shape, then break out the square and heave it over the side. The dogs romped below, occasionally getting thumped by the flying blocks.

We stopped for an afternoon ski up to Thoreau II. The cabin is so tiny that the roof took only an hour to shovel clear, but we could not stay because there was still more work to do at the larger camp. We went back for supper and shoveling. Though aching from the unaccustomed work, Mike was determined to finish the job that night. He wanted to spare my wrist, and besides, he had to be back next afternoon to cover the emergency room. After fortifying ourselves with steaks, baked potatoes, winter squash with maple syrup, and a chocolate chip cake, we pulled our heavy clothing back on and stepped out into a fifteen-degree night. It was totally still. A full moon probed with icy fingers through the tall spruces. The cold took our breaths away. We climbed back on the roof, and each started shoveling a new section. Fragrant smoke from the wood stove curled straight up in the frosty air toward superstars that sparkled outrageously.

I was bent over my shovel, back to the moon, when suddenly the shadow of a wolf fell across the roof. Huge, pointed ears and a bristling neck ruff lay directly under my shovel. I shrieked and straightened up so abruptly that I almost fell off the edge into a deep drift below. Whirling, I saw Condor silhouetted against the moon as he sat on the *peak* of the cabin. He had felt lonesome, apparently, down in the darkened woods and had climbed fifteen feet up the snowslide hill to join us. When Mike heard my shriek and saw Condor, *he* almost fell off the roof, laughing. "White

Fang has found us!"

Even after our job was done, I could not sleep. The moon was too compelling. Mike and the dogs had collapsed, and all were snoring loudly. Silently I slipped into boots and down parka and "cronched" over the snow onto the lake. On impulse I lay down spread-eagle and gazed up at the moon. The ice was working. It rumbled and cracked and thickened imperceptibly beneath my body. I felt as if I were lying in the pulsing, frigid palm of a giant.

A satellite went wandering past, blinking regularly. In my mind I leaped up beside it and looked down at myself lying on this thin layer of frozen water, sustained only by the thin layer of oxy-

The dogs and I share a peaceful moment in the snowy Adirondack woods.

gen between ice and stars. I made no more impression on this frozen surface than a water strider resting on the lake in summer. It took so little to buoy us up, yet both ice and air were perilously thin compared to the vastness of space about us.

My mind's eye peered through the ice into the water below— thirty-four degrees Fahrenheit, turgid, sluggish, greenish black. Nothing moving, except perhaps in the bottom mud a few crayfish crawled and bullheads nuzzled around in that arctic world. On impulse, I swept my arms through the snow up and down, as I'd done hundreds of times as a child, creating an "angel." A living, breathing angel. That was my response to the vast, cold universe above and beyond Black Bear Lake.

I started to shiver. I pictured how long it would take to turn me from hot-blooded living flesh to cold frozen protoplasm staring sightlessly at the satellites and stars, those implacable glimmers in the sky. It might be a good way to die if ever the need for suicide arose. But right now the thought of my downfilled loft, the toasty stove, and the warm body of my love drew me back into myself. I scrambled up and ran back to West of the Wind.

On my third trip it was late March—sunny, breezy, and beautiful—the tail end of winter, the last of it I'd see this year. The temperature stood at thirty degrees Fahrenheit. A cool north breeze swayed the balsams and sent old snow clumps dropping to the forest floor. The branches bobbed up, seemingly glad to be free of their winter burden. Finally I could stay at Thoreau II. As I snowshoed past the outlet of Lilypad Lake, the gurgle of water met my ears. It was flowing over the old beaver dam, newly released from the cold's prison. The ice was yielding. Though ten inches still floated on the lake's watery core, the edges were melting back from the shores. Winter was releasing the lake from its handcuffs with the land.

Out in front of the point, signs of an otter made a Morse code of pawprints, tail swipes, and belly glides in the snow. Here he'd step-step-stepped; there he'd glided. Then a step-step-glide-step-step-glide. Another three weeks, and he'd be doing water ballet.

That evening the aurora borealis played faintly in the northern horizon while the temperature dropped to five degrees. I stoked up my potbellied stove, then went out on the ice to watch. The North Star was still high. Mighty Orion still strode masterfully across the western quadrant of the sky. But he hadn't long to hunt. Spring was somehow in the air. This chionophobe could count on the fact that soon peepers would be trilling from blackwater barren-looking bogs. The yellowthroats and redstarts would come flitting through fresh, feathery tamaracks. Loons would be yodeling and courting on chill blue lakes. We would have all made it safely through another Adirondack winter. Especially me— *without* white fingers!

18

One Woman's Wilderness

W *Why do I continue* to bumble through the woods at night on mushy snow? Carry impossible loads by backpack and canoe? Go for backcountry saunters rather than shopping mall sprees? Cut and split firewood instead of turning up a thermostat? Build a little cabin to write at instead of buying a condo to relax in?

Perhaps it's because the world around me seems to be so complex and materialistic. It's my small rebellion to keep myself in pioneerlike fitness, to promote creativity, and to maintain a sense of adventure in my life. It's also my desire to exist in tune with sound ecological and ethical principles—that is, "small is beautiful," and "simplicity is best."

Much, much has changed since I bought a piece of wild forest beside Black Bear Lake, built my one-room cabin, and moved in with the idyllic notion of writing and living frugally and tranquilly. However, my way of life is still Spartan. I have no electricity and don't want any. I own no TV and don't want one. My radio, phonograph, and CB set are battery-operated. I still heat

In a stressed world we all need a private place. This is mine.

with wood stoves and continue to carry water from the lake in buckets. A daily swim is a must—in season. Two recent concessions are a gas hot-water heater for my tub and a generator to run a vacuum cleaner. I depend on an elaborate mail delivery system for most communication, even business stuff, although the phone machine across the lake serves in rush situations. I still use an outhouse.

But my professional life is far from simple or frugal. Expenses, particularly for insurance, taxes, film, developing, postage, and outdoor equipment, have skyrocketed. After a number of bizarre accidents my medical coverage is also high. But I dare not be without this insurance. My life-style is occasionally in the high risk category. In addition, with an increasing need to house more books, files, photo slides and albums, tents, sleeping bags, and so forth, I had to enclose the front porch and build an extra desk there. In so doing, I installed a sliding glass door, so that visitors would no longer have to squeeze through a window to gain access to that room. Later I added a basement storage area for files and a tool-gear shed and decided to enlarge my kitchen to include a dining table with four high stools. It wasn't fair to ask guests to eat on a desk littered with manuscripts, paper, and pens or in a rocking chair.

As for tranquillity, the lot of a free-lance writer/photographer/lecturer living in the woods is nothing like what I envisioned. I've gotten caught up in a giddy merry-go-round and (sometimes) rat race of assignments. I race to meet deadlines, to send out queries for new jobs, prepare for and drive to lecture engagements, edit photos, cajole or argue with editors, negotiate for fees and travel expenses, and attend conferences. The fact that I'm surrounded by deep forest and have black bears for neighbors doesn't alter the professional whirlwind inside my cabin. Life at West of the Wind is rarely serene. My very work *about* nature keeps me from the things I love to do *in* nature.

How did this all happen? Looking back to 1971, the year I began free-lancing, makes me chuckle. I started out with three thousand dollars in the bank. That's all—no alimony and no dividends coming in. I calculated that these savings would keep me for a year, even if I sold no articles or photos. My pal Rob reckoned he managed on thirty-five hundred dollars a year. His home was paid for, as was his car, but he drank five hundred dollars worth of liquor annually. I had no outstanding debts and didn't drink, so three thousand seemed reasonable. Furthermore, there was no overhead in my hand-built studio: no mortgage; no electric or phone bills. Water, heat, and entertainment (the great out-doors) were free with just a little muscle power. I owned an excel-lent reference library—books about nature and ecology, a thesau-rus, a dictionary, and well-thumbed copies of the *Writer's Market* and *Photographer's Market.*

That first year I sold a few short articles and wrote a child's book of bird folk tales. My income was barely enough to survive on, but my savings stayed intact. So I decided to try another year of free-lancing. By the third year I had started to feel established. In response to my many query letters, a number of article assign-ments came in, as did some consulting jobs in Central America and the Caribbean. The grueling self-discipline was second nature now. The post office was my second home. Gradually my publica-tions list lengthened and my contacts in the publishing and con-servation world expanded.

Each of my publications or consulting jobs seemed to lead to new ones. The writing of *Woodswoman,* for example, led to an-other book, *Assignment: Wildlife,* about the wildlife and wild-land conservation work I did away from the cabin, from the same publisher. Another publishing house then requested that I write *Women and Wilderness.* That text is being used in many college courses, in women's studies and American literature. Often these colleges invite me to come and lecture. And so it goes. . . .

What this proves to me is that once a person is set on a deter-mined course and perseveres, she or he can usually succeed. Today the proof of this belief is in my publications list. It includes four adult books, five children's books, five *National Geographic* arti-cles, and more than a hundred scientific and popular articles. Yet not so many years ago I could not fill half a page with references to anything I'd written.

The spin-offs of free-lancing have been surprising: equipment sponsorship; a demanding reader correspondence; membership in the Outdoor Writers Association of America (for which one must be extensively and currently published) and in the Explorers Club (for which one needs formal sponsorship). I've also recently been asked to do a magazine column for *Adirondack Life,* featuring monthly or bimonthly topics on nature and the environment in our park. Chekika and Condor are with me on the masthead photo, much to my delight.

There have also been numerous newspaper and TV interviews and a rare party or two. Not exactly the life of an Adirondack recluse, and not exactly a social butterfly. Usually there's enough public commitment and distraction to make me cherish the quiet, private times.

I plan to continue writing, lecturing, and consulting. It seems the best way to educate people about existing environmental problems and to nourish their love of nature. Besides, now that I have my little retreat and can return more often to backcountry basics, I tolerate outside intrusions better.

A lot of people fantasize about my life as a wilderness woman. The comments I hear most often are: "What do you do all day long?"; "Why I thought you'd be an Amazon—six feet two inches, a hundred seventy-five pounds, and bulging muscles"; "How do you manage to stay alone in the woods? I'd be scared silly," followed by "Don't you get awfully lonesome?" To some of these people the wilderness is a threatening place, full of loneliness and fear. To others it can be handled only by huge, burly, introverted men.

Others simply marvel that I built my own home and established a career. I try to tell them it was a natural progression of events. My professional training in ecology and conservation directed me to live close to wild places. My creative urge toward nature writing and photography demanded a quiet studio in which to work. Becoming a woodswoman was merely an extension of being an ecologist and a nature writer. In the wilderness I could *experience* the web of life rather than just understand it from books.

Actually I believe it would be much harder for a small-town woman to go to a city to pursue a career as a surgeon, TV anchorwoman, or stock analyst than to become a woodswoman. For me, the urban habitat and atmosphere would be far harder to deal with emotionally and much more dangerous physically than the wilderness.

How does it feel to be an unmarried woman in mid-life? Basically I like who I am, what I do, how I feel, and where I'm going. Since there's no way to bring back deceased parents and relatives or to create nonexistent brothers and sisters, I substitute friends for family. And I do have wonderful friends.

As for marriage, I don't think it would work for me now. I've gradually had a 180-degree change of attitude toward matrimony. Much as I adore Mike, I enjoy being single. It feels right. For now. Maybe ten years from now I'll come full circle and want to settle down. I believe Mike and I each need too much freedom and are too independent to succeed at marriage. Just as he needs to be unhampered by a demanding wife and kids in order to attend to patients' needs day or night, so I need to be in the wilds for extended periods to work and sustain my writing and environmental activism. A jealous or possessive husband would certainly cramp my style.

The mystiques of medicine and of ecology are very similar. One strives to make people healthy; the other, to keep the environment sound. Both demand strict discipline and a lifetime dedication. There's not a lot of free time for shared hobbies, fun, vacations.

All this is not to say I do not want, and do not have, a serious commitment. Two hardworking professionals can make a great combination, provided there's plenty of respect, flexibility, tolerance, compassion, and affection. You don't have to live continuously with someone to feel loved and cared for.

Sure I get lonesome—sometimes. But as I once described in *Woodswoman,* I felt more solitary and estranged during two winters in Washington, D.C., than I ever have in the woods. Macadam streets, soaring skyscrapers, and nameless crowds of faces always alienate me, whereas the outdoors, with its silence, wildlife, big trees, and starry skies, eases any loneliness. Just sitting on my dock through a summer's eve, watching otters cavort, and snowshoeing in a marshmallow white woods on a nippy winter day give me the sense of belonging to something vital and bigger than myself. Backcountry is the best place to feel useful, resourceful, vibrant, and whole.

Solitude in the wild forces me to call on inner resources. I like that. When a busy day's work is done, I can't flick on a color TV, call up Mike long distance, drive to a restaurant, or take in a movie. Instead, I watch a sunset, read by candlelight while rain drums on the roof, listen to good music on the radio, or write letters to friends. I make lists of things to tell Mike when I *do* get to phone or see him. There's seldom a boring moment.

As Irma Kurtz, in an article for *New Woman* about the "joy of solitude," says: "The key to true happiness lies with your abiilty to be alone." She also says, "Loneliness is the space within where once there was something or maybe someday there will be something. Nobody can 'cure' a space; all we can do is try to begin to fill it with something sustaining."

Yes, I get scared—sometimes. When winds thrash the big spruces above my cabins, I'm very nervous. While running my chain saw alone at Thoreau II, I fret about cutting a foot off and bleeding to death. And a long-term fear and anxiety is whether I'll be able to keep in good enough shape, physically and mentally, to chop wood, carry water, and backpack at age seventy-five . . . eighty-five?

I would hate myself if I ever got fat, stared at TV every night, and sat in a passive park by day. I'd despise any home where I had to take an elevator to reach it, open a burglarproof lock, throw garbage down a chute, or flick on fluorescents. After the life I've led? No way!

My biggest nightmare is of getting some crippling disease or condition with a progressive deterioration. I worry that such a catastrophic illness might force me to sell my cabins, dogs, and equipment. At the worst, debilitating illness would mean leaving the cabins and abandoning my life-style to seek health support systems. I also shudder at the modern technology that can keep one alive too long—not just the technology but the current mentality that approves of such an unnatural act.

To control this, I've made out a Living Will and attached it to my regular last will and testament. Mike and my lawyer know that I do not wish to be kept alive through heroic measures, nor do I want to exist as a vegetable. I've explained this as well to the two women friends who witnessed my will. (At the same time I signed forms donating my eyes, kidneys, and any other useful organ to science.)

Should misfortune strike, I would hope to have some say over continuing or ending my life. When a hunter finds an injured buck with an arrow in its hip, festering and gangrenous, he doesn't hesitate to shoot the animal quickly and cleanly. And when I discover a mouse or vole caught by its broken paw in one of my mouse traps in the kitchen, I rap it on the head with a spoon swiftly and neatly. There's no kindness in prolonging its agony, and I know of no vets who set mouse legs.

Similarly, I would like the option to choose death over being shorn of dignity. I still remember how Rob was kept alive artificially for weeks when he had willed himself to die. While I do not outwardly advocate committing suicide, I do believe there's a certain nobility in taking your own life when conditions are incurable or irreparable, provided it is done with consideration for those who will be left behind and while you are of sound mind.

Finally, I would choose to complete the circle of life here at my cabin. This is where I started so timidly and tentatively and where I evolved into a mature and productive woodswoman. Besides, I want to know that my energy as ashes will enter the earth, just as Pitzi's did, to be recycled into new life.

Does being childless bother me? Not at all. I can honestly say that I don't miss having children. I'm aware that not many women will agree with me. However, my life has been so rich, varied, and exciting—largely because I was *not* tied down as a mother and homemaker—that there can be no regrets. I have many small friends to love and cuddle and two goddaughters to dote on. Besides, German shepherds make wonderful child substitutes.

I also frequently have the opportunity to interact with high school and college-age people, especially young women, during my lectures and workshops. I love to see their bright, hopeful eyes as they ask questions about the best colleges for careers in ecology, how to build a cabin, or where to do research on rare and endangered wildlife. These young people have enough idealism and energy to put the whole world to rights. I enjoy counseling and encouraging them, almost like a parent, for I was in their shoes not too long ago. If young adults can be shown how to protect the environment and how to live honest, self-fulfilling, simple lives, that makes me feel like a good earth mother.

To this end, I've already established that half my estate should go to a Woodswoman Scholarship Fund at Cornell University's Department of Natural Resources. It will assist needy students, especially women working toward their master or doctoral degrees. The other half will probably go to set up a wildlife conservation fund, administered by a leading conservation organization like the World Wildlife Fund. My idea is that the fund will make small research grants available to well-qualified conservationists and biologists who wish to work in Latin America and the Caribbean—my favorite ecological consulting areas. The only catch is they must speak the language of the host country.

And if all goes well financially, I'd like to start a charitable corporation for the same purpose during my lifetime. In this way I can help young people *and* the environment and feel good about it. These budding conservationists can be my kids-students-colleagues all at the same time. These are the ways I am trying to reach out from my woodland retreat to embrace our modern generation and earth's ecological concerns.

19

Night Thoughts

Late at night I often canoe on Lilypad Lake. I may feel warm in my down bag and decide to cool off under the stars. Or a problem may leave me sleepless, twisting and turning up in the loft. Whatever. I always find a touch of tranquillity as I glide over the still black water, whether at 10:00 P.M. or 2:00 A.M.

In the fall I may wake to the sound of geese migrating and hope to catch a glimpse of them in the night sky. Then I float motionless, straining to see their silhouettes against a crescent moon as salmon as a native brook trout's belly. When flat night clouds sail across the moon, darkening the lake and landscape, I look back to my tiny cabin, where two candles burn as beacons. Thoreau II glows as softly as fox fire amid the inky forest.

In a way I am sorry to have diluted and disturbed the wilderness of this shoreline. Yet it has been such a small and loving intrusion, done with such a gentle, careful touch, that I'm sure the forest gods don't mind.

Building Thoreau II and living like Thoreau have given me the time, place, and serenity to search for answers to some philo-

Lilypad Lake, from the cabin window.

sophical questions. Certain thoughts keep crossing my mind as I slip over the lake's smooth surface, thoughts that have to do with the paradoxical quality of nature and, at times, its irony.

Here on the surface of the lake and above it reflections appear perfect, ripples create artistry. The water is clear and cold. It invites me to drink deeply, to trail fingers, to swim. Here, too, the surface is doing its job; water evaporates into the air and will later fall back as rain and dew. Ducks find a night's rest on Lilypad, while beavers ply their watery trails to find food. By day the lake seems pure and asparkle, at night, lovely and safe.

Yet I am aware of the underside of that surface, the water itself, the lake's bottom. The ultraclear water is the result of acid rain. From time to time great bubbles of hydrogen sulfide belch out of the gray-green algal mat at the bottom of the lake. If I enter the lake, the fetid muck will begin to suck me down, coat my bare feet with slime, and hamper me from kicking free to swim. The underworld of Lilypad is the exact opposite of its aboveworld.

The lake, I reflect, is like my life and the lives of many other people. There are two quite different aspects. Living here in a cabin seems healthy and carefree. In some ways it is. Yet there is that grasp of professional demands and public curiosity. There are the intrusions of mail, jets, and boats. There is the fracturing of silence. Also, the slow corrosion of my roof, pollution of water, and insidious poisoning of trees, fish, frogs, and maybe me. Ironically my life today seems a contradiction of how it was when I first came to Black Bear Lake.

Recognizing this duality, I realize more strongly than ever that the only way to handle this ambivalence is to fight the dark side—whatever it is—with short, sharp, intelligent skirmishes. Then you retreat, rest, and restore yourself in quiet, beautiful places. Thus you can gain strength and inspiration for the next battle. Perhaps that's why Thoreau wrote: "In Wildness is the preservation of the World."

Thoughts of sporadic struggle remind me of migrating monarch butterflies. The monarchs are the fragile gliders that go with the wind, stop with the cold. On chilly days you can see them clinging in torpid stupor to old goldenrod or milkweed stalks. They wait for the sun and a south wind to warm their wings and muscles for flight. Solo, each one seems to flutter dreamily toward its winter resting place against incredible odds, traveling up to two thousand miles at times.

Often they fly along or over highways. I see them being smashed by speeding cars. Although I purposely slow down when I'm driving, I sometimes hit them, too. A half ton truck moving at fifty-five miles an hour is a formidable butterfly killer. One minute the gossamer-winged orange insect is wafting down the East Coast toward Mexico; the next, there is a splat and a yellowish gob of goo is left on my windshield. Once I counted all the dead monarchs along a roadside as I drove through the Adirondacks. Even on this little-traveled route, they averaged five dead per mile. And that didn't count the goo spots on car windows and hoods.

If you multiply that number by all the miles of highway in both eastern and western Canada and the United States along which migrating monarchs may pass, the death toll is staggering. It almost seems impossible that any chrysalis can hatch, produce a delicate glider, and that it will ever arrive in either Pacific Grove, California, or the state of Michoacán, Mexico, at a ten-thousand-foot elevation, to winter with tens of thousands of the same species.

Moreover, the butterflies become dazed by TV, radio, and radar waves in the air. They can be zapped by insecticides and fertilizers on the ground. And in both California and Mexico their ancestral wintering grounds are being invaded by housing developments and agricultural projects and logging jobs. Where they do still find winter roosts, they crowd together until it is time to fly north in spring.

Obviously many monarchs make it. Yet the butterflies raise questions in me: Is the death of one monarch a chance event in a chaotic world? Or is there a pattern? Does a fate oversee them—or us? When a butterfly starts south, it can't call up the nearest weather station or the AAA to inquire about travel and road conditions. Does it have the slightest inkling of the many dangers that could lead to obliteration?

Then I think of the migrating geese. Those great gray wings pushing southward and the congregational honking of birds traveling together are one of the most exhilarating events I know of in nature. Wild geese are one of the few creatures that remind humans of the natural ties we have with other places, other states, other lands. They pull us out of ourselves. Geese give us a time frame to pace our lives by. Twice a year, at the two most critical seasons of life and death (spring and fall), the birds skim over our lives. They symbolize freedom, endurance, unity, commitment, wildness, and faith: faith that they will arrive where they want to go and perhaps the faith that each of us will attain our goals, too.

The ways of geese are different from those of butterflies. Geese are not dreamers but determined, hardworking migrants that use group dynamics, careful surveillance, age-old instincts, and memory to arrive at their destination. Many perish. But many still make the trip safely.

Even so, my exhilaration over their flight is short-lived. It is replaced by anxious imaginings. I thrill, then shiver as each flock flies over my canoe, for I know too much of what lies ahead once they leave the relative safety of our Adirondack Park.

Here, over Black Bear Lake—when they are one, two, three days out of Canada—the birds often falter. A glint of setting sun may show up on camp roofs and docks, discouraging the flock from landing. (How are they to know there's only me and two dogs around at this time of year? That none of us would do them harm?) They beat back up into the sky to seek a less populated body of water.

By dark they are nearing the Great Sacandaga Reservoir in the southern Adirondacks at an altitude of two thousand feet. Abruptly two F-14 jets from a Vermont air base zoom across their flight path. Although the geese are a mile away, the turbulence gently wobbles their V formation. The shriek of the turbines drowns their constant gabbling. They spiral into Sacandaga for the night.

At dawn they head southeast, passing over Albany, New York, and the Hudson River. Oil slicks, PCBs, sewage, and bilge water from the banana boats and oil barges have made the once-crystal Adirondack flow murky. It's unfit for goose or human.

The flock nears Boston by afternoon, traveling at a steady speed of fifty miles per hour. The leader, a gander, sees a pond, blue-green, deep and clear, surrounded by five hundred acres of woods, where all else is cement buildings, houses, and serpentine highways. Walden Pond seems safe and serene on this nippy October day. They land.

Two sentinel geese stand guard, unsure of the city sounds around the little state park. They stretch their long black necks with the white cheek patches, straining to detect danger. How are they to know that Walden is visited by half a million people each year? One sentinel glimpses joggers along the footpath encircling the pond. Instantly alert, he honks. The leader warns the group. The geese gather themselves up and flap into the twilight sky.

I picture them heading south now. One hundred and twenty pairs of wings, each with a six-foot span, eat up the distance. By dawn they reach New Jersey and the backlash of an October hurricane raging up the East Coast. Many are blown into the tall TV, microwave, and high-tension towers bristling across the state. Throughout central New Jersey the group finds no place to rest. Toxic waste sites, polluted swamps, transmission lines, belching factories mar the landscape. The gander veers east again, taking the flock close to New York City. A wave of warm air billows up to touch their pumping breasts—like a thermal—and push them higher. It's the bubble of heat above the city. Ashimmer with lights, Manhattan frightens and disorients the geese.

Later the birds are enticed by the Brigantine National Wildlife Refuge at the tip of New Jersey. Thousands of waterfowl are bobbing on the waters below, seemingly at ease. Weary with fatigue, the leader drops down, and the flock spends several days recuperating at this famous sanctuary with countless other migrants.

Back on their route, they bivouac at Chesapeake Bay, downstream from a large chemical plant. The water tastes bitter when the birds drink. Some have stomach cramps that night and cannot feed. The next day the geese come close to Washington, D.C.

Visibility lessens. Soon it is so poor that the birds cannot see the land from their normal flying altitude. They drop lower over the Chesapeake. Still smoggy.

Disobeying an age-old instinct to stay high, the gander brings his group into shotgun range of a poaching gang. Waterfowl season is not yet open, but the poachers hope to bag wild game for an illegal meat market that sells to high-priced restaurants up and down the coast.

Several shots ring out. Shotgun pellets rip through goose down, red muscle, and ivory bone; through bright goose eyes; through sturdy goose legs and sensitive goose beaks. Within two minutes half the flock is wounded or dead. The gander is one of the first to go. The remainder flap out over open water and disappear into the smog.

They head down the edge of Virginia and the Carolinas. An experienced female now leads. Maintaining their V formation all day, by dusk the birds look down on Barnwell, South Carolina, one of the two federally approved high-level nuclear waste disposal sites in the United States. A strange sensation quivers through the lead goose, then seems to pass to each bird down the lines. Their honking increases. Their electromagnetic fields, so sensitive and critical for navigation, feel skewed. Who knows what mysterious force radiates from those tens of thousands of tons of radioactive materials shallowly buried beneath the ground?

The next morning the sun is hot upon the great gray wings. As the geese approach the barrier islands of Georgia, acre upon acre of *Spartina* salt marsh, among the richest of ecosystems on earth, spread out below in a tawny-green carpet. Tidewater creeks meander darkly through the grass, brimming with fish, crustaceans, aquatic insects, and zooplankton. A national seashore park and several state refuges line the golden coast. Sea turtles nest there safely and seabirds thrive. The female feels a sense of homecoming. The geese descend. Of the original 120 birds, only 32 remain.

These, then, are my imaginings.

There are two ways to go through life and to attain your destination. You can waffle along like a beautiful dreamer or fly straight, high, and hard. Both methods have their share of dangers and pitfalls. But of the two, I choose the latter.

Why? Because though life is not a respecter of persons, I *do* believe that a portion of one's life *can* be manipulated and controlled by strength of character, persistence, goodwill, and determination. Comprehending so much more than butterflies and geese, humans can plan their routes, safeguard their movements, and even change their courses and goals if the going gets too rough.

It is crucial for me, living as I do, partially dependent on the caprices of nature and a free-lancing profession, to be in control of my life. Calvin Rutstrum says in his book *Back Country*, ". . . there is no morality in nature, that essentially it is amoral. But apparently there is some highly compensating factor in nature where capable conduct seems to be rewarded . . ."

Since time immemorial species have made special adaptations. I think each human should devise her or his special balance between determined action and quiet expectation. And he or she should live with the best of clean technology and natural simplicity.

Once I saw the crescent moon silhouette the spires of spruces and was struck by how sensuous nature can appear. However, I have had the opposite experience during a total eclipse of the moon in Guatemala in the 1960s and again in the Adirondacks in July 1982. On both occasions the moon suddenly seemed suspended like a circle of cold steel held in place by centrifugal force.

For the first time I sensed the earth we live on as utterly mechanistic, regulated, unchangeable. It operates on great, fixed, implacable laws of physics.

As I canoe in the dark on Lilypad, I can feel those laws at work all around me. The constellations and moon slowly "rise" with our planet's rotation around the sun. The water purls over the beaver dam in pure response to gravity. The lake responds to air temperatures—freezing and thawing. The fir trees grow toward the sun, rather than away from it, obeying a positive phototropism, or response to light. Actually not one natural event occurs without following some biological, chemical, meteorological, or physical law. It may look romantic and sensuous to *me*, but there's nothing romantic or sensuous about *nature*. It's the law!

Sometimes I lie in the bottom of my canoe and stare up at the stars, trying to visualize not only the constellations but the quasars, pulsars, black holes, galaxies, supernovas, and asteroids that astronomers tell us also inhabit our universe. The Milky Way, with its two hundred million stars, seems so peaceful, yet scientists say it is a violent universe up there. In fact, A.D. 15,000,000, they predict, a companion star to our sun will probably come so close to Earth that it will kill everything on it. It seems to me that a lot of things can go wrong in space if the laws don't operate right. There's nothing moral or compassionate about the universe. It's the law!

And yet . . . and yet . . . is this really the truth? We know that humans, and some animals, can be idealistic, affectionate, loyal, and even whimsical. Those characteristics don't arise from physics. So again I come to the conclusion that humans may have some sort of power and predetermination over their lives.

If this is so, then we should work unwaveringly toward our dreams and goals. There *is* hope that each of us can improve our lives, our environments, and the overall qualities of life. I'm going to function on this premise. I shall live deliberately in my beloved

Adirondacks. It's the best possible place for me. Here is West of the Wind, from which I'll fight environmental battles, and Thoreau II, to which I'll retreat for solace. Here are the beavers I swim with, the white-throated sparrows that wake me at dawn, the barred owls hooting me to sleep. Here, too, are the black bears and red squirrels that the dogs love to chase up trees. Rob is buried nearby. Old friends are near—Rod, Sid, and Sally—and I have Mike. While I know he'll never be a woodsman (you can't always find a complete package in one person), he has wonderful qualities of steadfastness, sobriety, reliability, and generosity.

I know I can cope with environmental changes, personal intrusions, and professional demands as long as I have my pocket of privacy and peace.

If you want inner peace, find it in solitude, not speed.
And if you would find yourself,
Look to the land from which you came
And to which you go.

—Henry David Thoreau

ABOUT THE AUTHOR

ANNE LABASTILLE is a wildlife ecologist and consultant with a doctorate from Cornell University. She is a commissioner of the Adirondack Park Agency, director at large of the National Wildlife Federation, and an honorary consultant to the World Wildlife Fund. She is also a Fellow of the Explorers Club, from which she received a citation of merit in 1984; and a registered New York State guide.